CLAIRE THOMSON
@5oclockapron

One Pan
BEANS

Creative Recipes Using Beans,
Chickpeas and Lentils for
Everyday Meals

photography by Sam Folan

quadrille

For Grace, Ivy and Dot –
heroic recipe testers all three

Introduction

Beans, and by extension pulses, are having a moment, which makes their turn in the spotlight sound short-lived, but it shouldn't be. Civilization has long relied on pulses as a primary and sustainable food source. Agriculturally, pulses are relatively stress-free to grow and easy to harvest. A low-impact food source, pulses require less land, less water, and little or no fertilizer. The legumes branch of the pulse family, working with healthy soil bacteria, have the remarkable ability to take nitrogen from the air to enrich the soil, reducing the need for fertilizers. As food sources go, the pulse family have it all – extremely economical, they provide valuable nutrients for little cost. Pulses are full to bursting with macronutrients, protein and fibre, while iron, potassium and folate are also present. Within a global food system, pulses are an efficient way to feed – and to fill – many. We only have to look to countries such as India, Spain, Niger, Brazil, the US, Italy, Tanzania, UAE, Israel, Mexico, Cuba and the UK (the leading pulse-eating countries in the world) to know that there is an abundance of pulse-proficient cookery that we can familiarize ourselves with, should we wish to.

When it comes to the human diet, no one size fits all (and never will) and vegetarians, vegans, pescatarians and carnivores all need to be accounted for, as do those with competing and often serious dietary requirements. Factor in the cost of ingredients, the different cookery facilities we all have access to and the amount of time and inclination we have to cook, and this topic is an enormous one. Thankfully, however, it is one where pulses are especially useful, their versatility and convenience a boon for any home cook.

With the credentials for eating more pulses undisputed and long accepted, I don't want to bog you down with too much detail in this short introduction. Suffice to say you can cook your pulses – be it beans, lentils, chickpeas and peas – from scratch, but you can also use jarred or canned pulses for all these recipes. This cookbook champions recipes from different pulse-eating countries and the recipes are all as delicious as they are faff-free to make.

The Oxford English Dictionary defines the word zeitgeist as 'the defining spirit or mood of a particular period of history as shown by the ideas and beliefs of the time'. If an ingredient can spearhead a zeitgeist, then let it be pulses, just arm yourself with one pan and get cooking.

A Word On Cooking With Pulses

I have written the recipes in this cookbook to work with dried pulses, which you will need to cook from scratch and, for convenience, pulses that come pre-prepared in various jars, cans, packets and pouches.

Firstly, let's talk dried pulses. As with most things sat on a shelf, time will hamper quality. Although dried, it is best to check the production date on any packets of dried pulses you buy. A short shelf life on a packet will ultimately mean a more desiccated ingredient, one that will take longer to rehydrate and to cook. Try and buy pulses from shops with a high turnover, this way you'll know the pulses are likely to have a longer shelf life on them, which is a good thing.

Generally speaking, the smaller the pulse, the shorter the cooking time, and while some pulses, like lentils or split peas, do not require soaking, if I have the time (even 15–30 minutes will do it), soaking these pulses will allow them to absorb water more evenly as they cook. Bigger pulses, beans for example, require soaking to ensure they cook evenly and, importantly, cut down the cooking time. Always soak pulses in a big enough container to submerge them fully in water as they soak, ideally about 4 hours for bigger beans. They will swell and you want them covered in water at all times, but you can always top up with more water if needed.

Some people will swear by the fact you must not salt the liquid in which you cook your pulses, but I don't believe this. Salt does not make for hard-to-cook pulses, in fact, I find an absence of salt in the cooking process will make for more tasteless pulses. The best way is to assertively salt your soaking liquid, drain, then fill a pan with fresh water with which you can then season more moderately to cook. I like to add aromatics to my cooking liquid – this can be as simple as a bay leaf and garlic clove, though could also include celery, carrots, slices of unwaxed lemon, onions, thyme, cinnamon sticks, whole dried chillies, I could go on. As a rule, look at a recipe and choose ingredients that feature should you want to ramp up flavour in your pulses as they cook.

Soaked pulses can be cooked on a stove top and simmered until tender, you can top up with more water if levels drop during the cook time. A lid will reduce this, but you will need to keep an eye on water levels and do give the pan a stir from time to time to prevent sticking. You can also braise beans in the oven. For this you will need a large high-sided baking dish, adding beans, water, salt and aromatics as above, then tightly seal to cook in a moderate to hot oven until tender. There are also some who swear by a pressure cooker as an energy-efficient and cost-effective way to cook pulses at home – I don't own one, but never say never. If in doubt, follow the cooking instructions on your packet of pulses, as for me to give an accurate cook time here that covers all pulses would be impossible.

As for how big a quantity you choose to cook, it's worth bearing in mind that if you're going to go to the trouble of cooking pulses from scratch, then do cook enough. Leftovers are a good thing and will last perfectly well if stored in the fridge for up to 3 days, plus they also freeze brilliantly. You can use the cooking water in lieu of any other liquids given in a recipe, especially if it tastes good.

Next up, pre-cooked and packaged pulses. These are an absolute lifeline, and I am in a panic if my cupboards are without at least one or another jar, packet, can or pouch. They are one of the most convenient fast foods around. There are plenty of brands around, some budget lines and some more pricey products. I have my favourites, and they come in a jar. Depending on the variety, taste the liquid and, if it tastes good, then use it! If it doesn't, then drain and season as you go. With this in mind, measurements for liquids needed in the recipes, and also the seasoning, will both need to be taken in to account.

And, finally, there is an abundance of pulses, so find your favourites and, honestly, if you prefer black beans to kidney beans or cannellini to butter (lima) beans, these recipes are a forgiving bunch, so use your judgement and enjoy the process.

SOUPS

Turkish Lentil Tomato Soup

Serves 4

4 celery stalks, finely chopped
1 onion, finely chopped
1 red (bell) pepper, deseeded and finely
    chopped
2 carrots, coarsely grated
4 tbsp olive oil, plus more to serve
3 garlic cloves, 2 finely chopped, 1 crushed
1 tbsp Turkish pepper paste or 2 tsp tomato
    purée (paste) mixed with 2 tsp unsmoked
    sweet paprika
1 tbsp ground cumin
1 x 400g (14oz) can chopped tomatoes
150g (5½oz) split red lentils, rinsed and drained
1 litre (35fl oz) vegetable stock or water
juice of ½ lemon
salt and freshly ground black pepper

To serve

100g (3½oz) plain yogurt
4 tbsp pumpkin or sunflower seeds (or a mix of
    both), ideally lightly toasted
1 tsp dried mint (optional)
1 tsp Urfa chilli flakes (optional)
flatbread or pitta (optional)

One of the quickest and easiest soups of all. Cook split red lentils, then slump into a soup that is sublime in texture, with no real need to blend. The soup's flavours take inspiration from Turkey, as does the serving suggestion of dried mint, chilli flakes and plain yogurt. I would suggest you serve this soup warm, not piping hot, for the flavours to really sing.

1. In a large saucepan over a moderate heat, cook the celery, onion, red pepper and carrots in the olive oil for 10 minutes until softened.

2. Meanwhile, mix the crushed garlic into the yogurt and season to taste with salt and pepper. Put to one side.

3. Stir the finely chopped garlic into the vegetables and cook for 1 minute until fragrant, then stir in the pepper paste and cumin and cook for 30 seconds.

4. Add the tomatoes and cook for 5 minutes to thicken, then stir in the red lentils, vegetable stock and salt and pepper to taste. Bring the mixture to the boil. Reduce the heat to low, cover and simmer for 20–25 minutes until the lentils are tender.

5. Use a stick blender, or a countertop blender, to partially purée half the soup until smooth and creamy. If using a countertop blender, work in batches and take care with the hot soup.

6. Return the puréed soup to the pan, add the lemon juice and adjust the seasoning if needed.

7. Ladle the soup into serving bowls and add a spoonful of the garlic yogurt. Sprinkle the seeds on top, with the dried mint and chilli flakes (if using), and finish with a drizzle of olive oil. Serve with wholemeal flatbread or pitta, if you like.

Lentil, Coconut and Peanut Butter Soup

Serves 4

250g (9oz) split red lentils, rinsed and drained
1 litre (35fl oz) vegetable stock or water
1 cinnamon stick
4 green cardamom pods
1 star anise
6 makrut lime leaves
1 tsp ground turmeric
3 garlic cloves, finely sliced
4 thin slices of fresh ginger
200ml (7fl oz) coconut milk
4 tbsp smooth peanut butter
2 tsp fish sauce, vegan fish sauce or soy
   sauce, plus more to taste
1 tsp palm sugar or soft light brown sugar
juice of ½ big lime
salt and freshly ground black pepper

To serve

70g (2½oz) roasted peanuts, roughly chopped
1 small bunch of coriander (cilantro), roughly
   chopped
1–2 green chillies (according to taste),
   finely sliced
40g (1½oz) crispy onions or shallots (optional)
½ big lime, cut into wedges

This recipe uses the ever-present staple of the storecupboard, split red lentils, which offer a speedy and satisfying cook. This recipe could not be any easier: simply boil the lentils with some turmeric and whole spices until soft, then add some coconut milk, lime and fish sauce along with a generous helping of smooth peanut butter to thicken and enrich. Serve with chopped coriander, a pebbledash of salted peanuts and lots of freshly chopped chilli and coriander.

1. Put the lentils in a large saucepan with the stock, along with the whole spices, lime leaves, turmeric, garlic and ginger. Bring to the boil. Skim off any froth that surfaces and simmer for 30 minutes until the lentils are cooked through and fallen apart.

2. Add the coconut milk and peanut butter and whisk to dissolve. Add the fish sauce, sugar, lime juice and a pinch of salt and pepper and taste, adding more fish sauce to taste if needed.

3. Serve topped with the peanuts, coriander, green chillies and crispy onions (if using) and a wedge of lime.

Dal Tadka

Serves 4

5 tbsp ghee or sunflower oil
4 small shallots, very thinly sliced
1 tbsp cumin seeds
1 tsp mustard seeds
1 tsp chilli flakes
20 curry leaves
400g (14oz) mung dal (skinned yellow split
　mung beans), rinsed and drained
4 garlic cloves, thinly sliced
4 thin slices of fresh ginger
2 tsp ground turmeric
4 small green chillies, or more or less to taste
salt

Dal Tadka is an Indian dish of cooked lentils and spices. There are many recipes for dal. I am using mung dal – skinned yellow split mung beans – for this recipe. Dal is a triumph in the cannon of one-pan cooking: make the tadka (spiced ghee or oil) before you begin the dal preparation, then use half to cook the dal, the spices permeating from the beginning of the cook time, and use the remainder to lace the top of the cooked warm dal, the smell of the spices used in the tadka sent reeling once more.

1. Heat the ghee in a large saucepan over a moderate heat and add the shallots, cumin seeds, mustard seeds and chilli flakes and cook until the shallots are golden. Stir in the curry leaves and warm for 1 minute. Carefully remove about half the oil, the seeds, shallots, chilli flakes and curry leaves to a bowl and put to one side.

2. Add the mung dal and cover with 1 litre (35fl oz) of water. Bring to the boil and skim off any scum that rises to the surface.

3. To the boiling dal, add the garlic, ginger slices, turmeric and ½ teaspoon of salt.

4. Turn down the heat, cover the pan, leaving the lid slightly ajar, and simmer very gently for about 45 minutes–1 hour, stirring occasionally, until the dal breaks down completely and becomes creamy, adding some boiling water if it dries out too much.

5. Add the whole green chillies and simmer for an additional 5 minutes.

6. Season to taste with salt and pour over the reserved oil along with the shallots, curry leaves and spices, then serve.

Rasam

Serves 4

500g (1lb 2oz) tomatoes, roughly chopped
3 tbsp tamarind paste
3 tbsp ghee or sunflower oil
2 tsp mustard seeds
10–12 curry leaves
2 garlic cloves, finely chopped
1 tsp ground turmeric
½ tsp chilli flakes, or more to taste
100g (3½oz) split red lentils, rinsed and drained
½ small bunch of coriander (cilantro),
   roughly chopped
salt and freshly ground black pepper

For the rasam powder
2 tbsp coriander seeds
1 tbsp cumin seeds
½ tsp mustard seeds
½ tsp fenugreek seeds
1 tbsp black peppercorns
4–5 dried red chillies
1 tbsp split red lentils
½ tsp asafoetida (hing)

Rasam is a hot and sour soup served in southern India. This recipe instructs you to make a rasam powder, which involves toasting the spices and the lentils in a pan to heighten their flavour and fragrance. You'll make more powder than this soup needs, so keep any unused powder in a container and use to make the soup once again. This soup is sour with tamarind and tomato and spiced with a comprehensive selection of spices and dried chilli, and I would argue all of them are necessary for a really good rasam.

1. For the rasam powder, dry roast all the whole seeds, the peppercorns, chillies and lentils in a large pan over a low heat for 3–4 minutes until they become aromatic, taking care not to burn them. Let them cool, add the asafoetida and grind into a powder, using a pestle or mortar (or you can give them a quick blitz in a mini food processor to form a coarse dust). Put in a bowl and leave to one side.

2. In a blender, blend half the tomatoes with the tamarind paste, 2 tablespoons of the rasam powder and salt and pepper to taste.

3. Heat the ghee in the pan over a medium heat. Add the mustard seeds and let them splutter. Add the curry leaves, garlic, turmeric and chilli flakes and cook for 30 seconds until fragrant.

4. Add the blended tomatoes and cook for 5 minutes to thicken.

5. Add the lentils and 1 litre (35fl oz) of water, bring to the boil, then cover and cook over a moderate to low heat for 30 minutes until soft. Add salt and rasam powder to taste.

6. Serve topped with the chopped coriander and a pinch more rasam powder, if you like.

Harira

Serves 4

600g (1lb 5oz) diced lamb (shank, neck, or shoulder)
2 tbsp olive oil
1 onion, finely chopped
3 celery stalks, finely chopped
2 garlic cloves, finely chopped
2 tbsp tomato purée (paste)
1½ tsp ground cumin
¼ tsp ground cardamom
½ tsp ground ginger
½ tsp ground turmeric
½ tsp ground cloves
1 cinnamon stick
1 bay leaf
300g (10½oz) tomatoes, diced (or used chopped canned tomatoes)
1 litre (35fl oz) chicken or lamb stock (or use water)
approx. 250g (9oz) drained cooked or canned chickpeas (garbanzos)
½ bunch of coriander (cilantro), leaves finely chopped
70g (2½oz) vermicelli pasta (or use broken spaghetti)
200g (7oz) brown lentils, soaked for 40 minutes and drained
salt and freshly ground black pepper

To serve
4 medjool dates, pitted and sliced (optional)
lemon wedges

Harira is a Moroccan one-pot stew made with lamb and a mix of beans or chickpeas as well as lentils. During Ramadan it is a popular dish to serve, rich and hearty, a dish of real sustenance. I was shown how to make this dish using lamb shanks cooked in a pressure cooker by a chef from a Spanish and Moroccan-inspired restaurant in London. Thinly sliced dates and lemons to squeeze is a traditional serving suggestion and one I urge you to use.

1. In a large pan over a moderate heat, cook the lamb in the olive oil until lightly coloured on all sides – about 15 minutes.

2. Add the onion and celery and cook along with the lamb for 5 minutes until softened.

3. Add the garlic and cook for 1 minute until fragrant, then stir in the tomato purée, ground spices, the cinnamon stick and the bay leaf. Cook for a few minutes to allow the spices to infuse.

4. Add the tomatoes and cook for 5 minutes until thickened, then add the stock and bring to the boil. Reduce the heat to low, season to taste with salt and pepper, then cover and simmer for about 1 hour, or until the lamb is tender.

5. Add the chickpeas, half the coriander, the vermicelli and soaked lentils and cook for about 30 minutes until the lentils are cooked. Check the seasoning, adding salt and pepper to taste.

6. Ladle the harira into bowls and top with the remaining coriander and the date slices, with lemon wedges on the side.

Black Bean Posole

Serves 4

3 dried ancho chillies, destemmed, deseeded
and soaked in boiling water for 5 minutes
1 onion, finely chopped
1 green (bell) pepper, deseeded and finely
chopped
3 tbsp coconut, sunflower or olive oil
3 garlic cloves, finely chopped
1 tsp Mexican or dried oregano
2 tsp ground cumin
2 bay leaves
400g (14oz) pork belly or shoulder, cut into
3–4-cm (1½–2-inch) cubes
approx. 500g (1lb 2oz) drained cooked or
canned black beans
juice of ½ lime, plus more to taste
salt and freshly ground black pepper

For the toppings
8 radishes, thinly sliced
1 avocado, peeled, stoned and sliced
1 small bunch of coriander (cilantro),
roughly chopped
2 fresh jalapeños, thinly sliced
a handful of tortilla chips
a few tbsp feta, finely crumbled (optional)
1 lime, cut into wedges

Pozole or posole is a classic Mexican soup made using beans and meat, often chicken or pork. The spelling deviates the closer you get to the US border – cooked in Mexico, the dish is spelt with a z. Traditionally, the dish might take several days to make and uses hominy – big starchy dried maize kernels. If you want to make this dish with hominy you will need more time than I give you here, but you can also take a shortcut and use canned hominy, though here in the UK this can be hard to come by. Instead, I have given this recipe using just black beans and pork among other ingredients. The serving suggestions are everything, so try to include as many as is prudent to source to top this hearty dish.

1. Drain the ancho chillies and thinly slice. Put to one side, reserving the liquid.

2. In a large deep pan over a moderate heat, cook the onion, half the ancho chillies and the green pepper in the oil for 10 minutes until soft. Add the garlic, oregano, cumin and bay leaves and cook for 1 minute until aromatic.

3. Add the pork and cook for 5 minutes, then add 800ml (28fl oz) of water and the chilli soaking liquid and bring to the boil. Reduce the heat to low, cover, and cook for 30–40 minutes until the pork is tender.

4. Stir in the beans and heat through, then remove from the heat and season with salt and pepper to taste, adding the lime juice.

5. Serve the black bean soup in bowls, topped with the remaining ancho chillies, the radishes, avocado, coriander, fresh jalapeños, tortilla chips and feta (if using), and with lime wedges on the side.

Minestrone with Cannellini Beans

Serves 4

75g (2½oz) pancetta, finely chopped
  (optional – add a couple more tbsp of
  olive oil if not using)
2 tbsp good extra virgin olive oil, plus
  more to coat the pasta
1 onion, finely chopped
1 large carrot, finely chopped
4 celery stalks, finely chopped
2 garlic cloves, finely chopped
6 stalks of rainbow chard, leaves sliced,
  stalks finely chopped
1 medium potato, peeled and cut into 2cm
  (¾in) dice
80g (2¾oz) little pasta shapes, or use
  risotto rice
1 litre (35fl oz) chicken or vegetable stock
2 bay leaves
1 big thyme sprig
2 firm courgettes (zucchini), finely chopped
250g (9oz) drained cooked or canned
  cannellini beans
salt and freshly ground black pepper

For the pesto
30g (1oz) bunch of basil, leaves picked and
  stalks reserved
1 garlic clove, finely chopped
3 tbsp extra virgin olive oil
30g (1oz) parmesan, finely grated, plus a bit
  more to serve

Ideally you will make the pesto to serve with this minestrone but, honestly, if you are pressed for time and spot some good-looking store-bought pesto, often found in the refrigerated aisle, by all means go for it, no one will mind. Use cannellini beans here (cooked from dried or canned, up to you) and while I list pancetta in the recipe, you could just as well do without it. The potato is essential, though, as what this peeled and diced potato brings to this one-pan bean dish is incalculable – bulk to break down and thicken the soup, bringing with it, along with the beans, a comforting and creamy heft. Concentrate on balancing the flavours here, there's a lot going on and, as ever, it is well worth the effort.

1. For the pesto, combine the basil leaves and garlic in a pestle and mortar or small blender to form a smooth paste. Stir in the olive oil and parmesan, then season to taste with salt and pepper. Put to one side.

2. In a large saucepan over a moderate heat, cook the pancetta in the olive oil for 3–5 minutes until the fat runs out and it becomes nicely coloured.

3. Add the onion, carrot and celery with a big pinch of salt and cook for 10–15 minutes until very soft and beginning to stick to the bottom of the pan. Stir in the garlic and cook for 1 minute until aromatic.

4. Add the chopped chard stalks, potato and pasta and stir together for 1 minute, then pour in the stock, add the bay leaves, basil stalks (reserved from the pesto) and thyme sprig and bring to the boil. Turn down the heat and simmer for 10 minutes until the potato and pasta are tender, then stir in the courgettes and cook for 2 minutes.

5. Add the sliced chard leaves and the cannellini beans. Cook for 2 minutes until piping hot and the chard is wilted.

6. Taste and adjust the seasoning with salt and pepper, if required, and remove the herbs.

7. Serve the minestrone topped with the basil pesto and with a bit more grated parmesan.

Italian Wedding Soup with Lentils

Serves 4

400g (14oz) good-quality sausages,
   skins removed
1 onion, finely diced
1 carrot, finely diced
2 celery stalks, finely diced
2 tbsp olive oil
1 garlic clove, finely chopped
1 litre (35fl oz) chicken or vegetable stock
60g (2¼oz) little pasta shapes
100g (3½oz) baby spinach
250g (9oz) drained cooked or canned
   green lentils
salt
finely grated parmesan, to serve

Not to be confused with a soup to serve on your wedding day, this dish is, after all, perhaps too wholesome an offering given such an auspicious and romantic day. In Italian, the name Minestra Maritata refers to the marriage of ingredients, specifically some meat and an abundance of leafy green vegetables. I've taken the liberty of adding some lentils and tiny pasta shapes to the broth, and I also suggest using some good-quality sausages for ease and speed (instead of making meatballs), creating a soup to enjoy 10, 20 years and more into a marriage, sitting opposite one another at the kitchen table, deeply and irrevocably in love.

1. Using wet hands, roll the sausage meat into small meatballs and set aside.

2. In a large pan over a medium heat, cook the onion, carrot and celery in the olive oil for 10 minutes until soft and rich, then add the garlic and cook for 1 minute until fragrant.

3. Pour in the stock and bring to a simmer. Add the pasta and sausage meatballs and cook until the pasta is al dente and the meatballs are cooked through, anywhere between 10–15 minutes.

4. Stir in the baby spinach and lentils and cook until the spinach is wilted and the lentils are piping hot.

5. Adjust the seasoning with salt and the consistency with additional stock, as required.

6. Serve topped with some finely grated parmesan.

Split Pea and Ham Soup

Serves 4

2 bay leaves

1 small bunch of parsley, leaves picked and finely chopped, stalks separated

1 big thyme sprig

400g (14oz) uncooked ham or bacon in a single piece

2 tbsp extra virgin olive oil

2 onions, finely diced

3 garlic cloves, finely diced

400g (14oz) carrots, thinly sliced

3 celery stalks, thinly sliced

400g (14oz) dried split green peas, rinsed and drained

salt and freshly ground black pepper

This soup goes by the fabulous name of London Particular; so called because the recipe was named after the 'pea souper' fogs of London back in the 1950s. It is made with dried split peas, some onion and a ham hock among other ingredients. The creamy depth of the cooked peas blitzed down with the smoked hock stock was thought to mimic the murky green fog, which at the time was so thick you could barely see your hand in front of your face. Back to this soup, granted, it's never going to be a looker, but it does have a great name and tastes fantastic to boot. I recommend using a piece of uncooked ham or you could use a piece of bacon, smoked ideally, to ape the more traditional ham hock – my way is speedier and easier.

1. Tie the bay leaves, parsley stalks and thyme sprig into a bundle with some string (alternatively leave untied and pick out later). Put to one side.

2. Place the ham or bacon in a large pan and cover with water. Bring to the boil, drain and discard the water, returning the empty pan to the heat.

3. Add the olive oil and the onions to the pan and cook over a moderate heat for 10 minutes until soft, then add the garlic and cook for 1 minute until aromatic. Add the carrots, celery and the herb bundle and cook for another 1 minute, stirring.

4. Nestle the ham or bacon into the vegetable mixture, then add the split peas and 1.5 litres (52fl oz) of water. Bring to the boil and reduce the heat to low. Cover and cook for 45 minutes–1 hour until the split peas have softened and cooked through in the soup mixture, stirring every 15–20 minutes.

5. Remove the ham or bacon from the soup and place it on a wooden cutting board. Remove any meat pieces from the hock and chop or pull the meat into roughly 2cm (¾in) pieces. Remove the herb bundle or herbs and discard.

6. Stir the pieces of meat into the soup, remove the pan from the heat, and immediately stir in the chopped parsley leaves. Season to taste with salt and pepper, then serve.

Chickpea and Chorizo Soup with Fried Bread and Eggs

Serves 4

80g (2¾oz) cooking chorizo, diced or sliced

3 tbsp olive oil

3 thick slices of rustic day-old bread (about 150g/5½oz), torn into approx. 1–2cm (½–¾in) pieces, plus more, toasted and rubbed with garlic, to serve

8 garlic cloves, finely chopped

1 small bunch of flat-leaf parsley, finely chopped, reserving a small amount to garnish

2 bay leaves

1 tsp sweet paprika (Spanish pimentón if possible)

1 litre (35fl oz) chicken stock

approx. 500g (1lb 2oz) drained cooked or canned chickpeas (garbanzos) – or use any white beans

4 eggs

salt and freshly ground black pepper

Try and buy proper Spanish chorizo and pimentón for this recipe. Cooking the chorizo to first render the fat in the pan with which you then toast the torn bread is transformative, and a winning way with stale bread. This cooked bread then goes on to make the soup, swelling and thickening the liquid along with the chickpeas, before you finally poach some eggs in the soup. This is a hearty dish – one I'd like everyone to make.

1. In a pan over a moderate heat, cook the chorizo in the olive oil for about 5 minutes until it is coloured and has released its fat.

2. Add the bread pieces to the pan and fry for 2–3 minutes, or until the bread has absorbed all the fat and begins to start toasting in places. Add the garlic, parsley, bay leaves and paprika and cook for 30 seconds. Pour in the stock, bring to the boil, then reduce the heat and simmer for 5 minutes. Add the chickpeas and simmer for 2–3 minutes until piping hot, then season to taste with salt and pepper.

3. Gently crack in the eggs, making sure they're all evenly spaced out, cover the pan and poach at a simmer for 3–4 minutes, or until the egg whites are fully cooked through.

4. Garnish with the remaining parsley and serve straight away with more toasted bread.

White Bean and Fennel Soup with Green Olive and Parsley Dressing

Serves 4

1 large onion, finely diced

2 fennel bulbs, trimmed and finely diced (any fronds reserved)

4 tbsp olive oil, plus extra for the dressing

3 garlic cloves, finely chopped

½ tsp ground fennel seeds

800ml (28fl oz) vegetable stock

approx. 250g (9oz) drained cooked or canned white beans of your choice

40g (1½oz) pitted green olives, roughly chopped

½ small bunch of parsley, finely chopped

finely grated zest of 1 unwaxed lemon

salt and freshly ground black pepper

White bean soups are among my favourites as they are supremely satisfying to make. In this recipe, I blend the soup until thickened and smooth, but if you prefer, you could just as easily blend only a portion of the soup, retaining a little texture, or blend none at all. I'll leave this up to you, it depends on my mood. Sometimes I am a fan of some chubby, fudgy beans wallowing in the flavoursome liquid, and sometimes I am not, blending the mix to smithereens. The green olive and parsley dressing gives just enough jazz to the soup but still keeps things simple.

1. In a large saucepan over a moderate heat, cook the onion and fennel in the olive oil for around 10 minutes until softened. Add the garlic and ground fennel, season well with salt and pepper and cook for 2 minutes more, until fragrant.

2. Add the vegetable stock and white beans to the pot. Bring the soup to a simmer and cook for 10–15 minutes to allow the flavours to meld and the soup to thicken.

3. Meanwhile, in a bowl, mix together the green olives, any reserved fennel fronds, the parsley and lemon zest and season to taste with salt and pepper. Stir in a tablespoon or so of olive oil to make a thick dressing.

4. Remove the soup from the heat and, using a stick blender, carefully blend until smooth. Alternatively, you can also partially blend or even not blend at all.

5. Check the seasoning, adding additional salt and pepper to taste. Serve topped with the green olive and parsley dressing.

STOVE
TOP

Ethiopian Split Pea Stew

Serves 4

60g (2¼oz) butter or ghee
4 garlic cloves, 1 thinly sliced, 3 finely chopped
5 green cardamom pods, lightly crushed
½ tsp fenugreek seeds
1 tsp cumin seeds, toasted
1 clove
2 bay leaves
200g (7oz) split yellow peas, rinsed and
    drained, plus an extra 2 tbsp
2 tsp berbere spice blend
1 red onion, thinly sliced
1 tsp ground turmeric
1 tsp ground cumin
1 tsp ground coriander
1 tsp ground ginger
1 tsp dried basil (optional)
200g (7oz) chopped tomatoes, fresh or canned
1 tbsp tomato purée (paste)
salt and freshly ground black pepper
1–3 green chillies, thinly sliced, to serve

The magic of this recipe is in the spiced butter, which is called niter kibbeh in Ethiopian cooking, spooned over the stew to scent and enrich, it is astonishing. I have taken inspiration for this recipe from Kik Alicha – an Ethiopian recipe, of which there are many different versions. Grinding some of the split peas into the spice blend thickens the stew and gives a pleasing, creamy texture. It is a technique also used in some Indian cooking, specifically dishes like sambar masala or rasam powders (see page 16). It is a cookery practice that I have found particularly useful when looking at world cuisines and global cookery methods.

1. Heat the butter or ghee in a saucepan over a moderate heat, add the sliced garlic, whole spices and bay leaves and cook for 2 minutes, or until the butter is fully melted. Put to one side to infuse for 30 minutes.

2. Use a pestle and mortar or small blender to grind 2 tablespoons of split peas and 1 teaspoon of the berbere to a coarse powder. Put to one side.

3. Warm and strain half the butter (discarding the garlic, bay and spices) back into a saucepan. Fry the onion in the spiced butter for 5 minutes, or until the onion is softened, then add the chopped garlic, the remaining berbere, the ground spices and the dried basil (if using) and cook for 30 seconds until fragrant.

4. Stir in the tomatoes, tomato purée and ½ teaspoon of salt and cook for 5 minutes, or until thickened.

5. Add the remaining split peas and 1 litre (35fl oz) of water and bring to the boil, then cover and simmer for 45 minutes until the split peas are tender (adding a splash of water if it needs it).

6. Stir in the berbere mixture, season to taste with salt and pepper and serve topped with green chilli.

Dal Makhani

Serves 4

400g (14oz) whole urad (black) or dark green
   speckled lentils
1 onion, finely diced
1 cinnamon stick
6 green cardamom pods, squashed slightly
3 black cardamom pods (optional, but add
   lovely deep and slightly smoky flavour)
2 bay leaves
4 dried red chillies
50g (1¾oz) butter or ghee
1 tbsp finely grated fresh ginger
4 garlic cloves, finely chopped
1 tbsp tomato purée (paste)
½ tsp smoked paprika
1 tbsp garam masala
½ tsp smoked salt (optional)
80g (2¾oz) plain yogurt (not Greek)
80ml (2½fl oz) double (heavy) cream
1 tsp dried fenugreek leaves (kasoori methi)
salt and freshly ground black pepper
rice, paratha, naan or chapati, to serve
   (optional)

This rich and luxurious restaurant-style dal is popular in the UK but has its origins in Punjabi cooking. The dried fenugreek in this recipe is worth seeking out, it is readily available online, in South Asian stores and in bigger supermarkets. Adding it at the end lends a grassy, smoky fragrance, and with the garam masala, the warmth of the finished dish sends these spices reeling. This recipe suits darker lentils and can also include kidney beans. Overall, the dish benefits from a long, slow cook time.

This dal should, when traditionally made, have a sense of smokiness to it, cooked as it sometimes was, and I suppose might still be, over an open fire. Cooking this dal here in my kitchen in Bristol, I'm aping this smoky flavour by using some smoked salt and smoked paprika, both optional but it's a strong recommendation to do so from me. Serve with rice, paratha, naan or chapati.

1. Soak the lentils in cold water for a few hours, then drain and rinse.

2. In a large saucepan over a moderate heat, cook the onion, whole spices, bay leaves and dried chillies in 25g (1oz) of the butter for 10 minutes until softened. Then add the ginger, garlic, tomato purée, paprika and half the garam masala and cook for 1 minute until fragrant.

3. Add the drained lentils, smoked salt (if using) and 1.2 litres (42fl oz) of water and bring to the boil. Turn down the heat and simmer gently for 45 minutes–1 hour, or until the lentils are cooked through.

4. Stir through the yogurt and the remaining butter and season to taste with salt and pepper. Serve topped with the cream and sprinkled with the remaining garam masala and the dried fenugreek leaves. Serve with rice or your choice or paratha, naan or chapati.

Black-eyed Bean Jambalaya with Chorizo and Chicken

Serves 4

600g (1lb 5oz) boneless chicken thighs

1 tsp hot smoked paprika

1 tsp ground cumin

½ tsp ground coriander

200g (7oz) smoked Polish cooking sausage or cooking chorizo, sliced

1 tbsp olive oil

3 celery stalks, finely chopped

1 green (bell) pepper, deseeded and finely diced

1 red (bell) pepper, deseeded and finely diced

1 onion, finely chopped

2 garlic cloves, finely chopped

1 tsp dried oregano

1 x 400g (14oz) can chopped tomatoes

200g (7oz) long-grain or basmati rice

450ml (16fl oz) hot chicken stock or water

2 x 400g (14oz) cans black-eyed beans (black-eyed peas), drained and rinsed

salt and freshly ground black pepper

Tabasco or hot sauce, to serve

Jambalaya has its roots in Creole and Cajun culinary traditions, influenced by Spanish, African and French cooking. It has numerous regional variations and is the subject of widespread debate in many different cookery communities. A common thread, however, is the incorporation of onions, celery and peppers, an essential base and the holy trinity in any authentic jambalaya. The addition of tomato denotes the dish as a red or Creole jambalaya, which is more typical in New Orleans. The inclusion of sausage is also important and would traditionally include Cajun andouille sausage, but given it can be tricky to source these sausages elsewhere in the world, I have suggested a spiced smoked sausage such as chorizo or smoked Polish kielbasa as an acceptable substitute. Black-eyed beans are not traditionally included in jambalaya, but under the multivarious umbrella of rice and legume dishes the world over, I have taken the liberty and added some to this jambalaya, because, where there's a great dish, one with world renown, and a bean can be squeezed in, well, why not?

1. Mix the chicken with the paprika, cumin and coriander and season with salt and pepper.

2. In a large frying pan (with a lid) over a moderate heat, fry the chicken and sausage or chorizo in the olive oil for about 5 minutes until the chicken is coloured all over.

3. Add the celery, peppers and the onion and cook for 10 minutes until softened.

4. Add the garlic and oregano and cook for 1 minute, then add the tomatoes and cook for 5 minutes until thickened.

5. Add the rice, stir well and cook for around a minute until the rice begins to turn opaque in the ends. Cover with the stock, cover with a lid, and cook over a medium-low heat for 20 minutes, then add the black-eyed beans, cover again and cook until the liquid is absorbed and the rice is cooked – about 5 minutes.

6. Allow to rest for 5 minutes before serving with the hot sauce.

Pasta e Fagioli

Serves 4

1 onion, finely diced
3 celery stalks, finely diced
1 carrot, finely diced
4 tbsp olive oil, plus more to serve
4 garlic cloves, finely chopped
1 tbsp fresh rosemary or sage leaves,
    finely chopped
1 tbsp tomato purée (paste)
1 litre (35fl oz) chicken or vegetable stock
100g (3½oz) small pasta shapes, such as
    macaroni, orzo or ditalini (I have had equal
    success with broken-up sheets of lasagne)
approx. 250g (9oz) drained cooked or canned
    borlotti beans
½ tsp chilli flakes (optional)
salt and freshly ground black pepper
parmesan, finely grated, to serve

Hands down this is a dish that has comforted me for as long as I have been cooking and feeding my family. It is my go-to dinner when I haven't been shopping for days and my desperate ransacking of the cupboards needs to manifest something out of nothing. You can also make this with lentils instead of beans, in which case it is called pasta e lenticchie. The combination of pulses and legumes and pasta is one of the most cost-effective ways to produce a nutritious and satisfying meal. The practice has roots in the so-called peasant cooking of Italy, in day-to-day terms, whatever your income and from wherever you are cooking in the world, it is prudent and sensible cooking practice. The dish can be thick like a stew or thinner like a soup. Fresh beans are a particular treat for this recipe, more costly too, but by all means use some when in season. As dishes go, this is one to let your best olive oil shine when it comes to plating up. And, finally, with so few ingredients, crucial to the success of this dish is to cook and caramelize the vegetables until sweet and concentrated before adding the liquid.

1. In a large pan over a medium heat, cook the onion, celery and carrot in the olive oil with a big pinch of salt for 10–15 minutes until very soft and beginning to stick to the bottom of the pan, stirring often.

2. Add the garlic and rosemary and cook for 30 seconds until fragrant, then add the tomato purée and cook for 5 minutes until thickened.

3. Add the stock and bring to the boil, then add the pasta and simmer until tender using the packet instructions as a guideline, adding the beans for the last 2 minutes to heat through.

4. Season the soup with salt and pepper and the chilli flakes (if using), then serve with plenty of grated parmesan and a drizzle of olive oil.

Chickpeas with Lamb, Saffron and Cumin

Serves 4

800g (1lb 12oz) lamb leg or loin, diced into
    3cm (1¼in) cubes
2 tsp smoked paprika
2 tsp cumin seeds, toasted and ground
2 tsp fennel seeds, ground
4 tbsp extra virgin olive oil
½ lemon
4 garlic cloves, finely chopped
1 onion, finely chopped
2 tbsp raisins (optional)
pinch of saffron
1 tbsp tomato purée (paste)
200g (7oz) baby spinach
approx. 500g (1lb 2oz) drained cooked or
    canned chickpeas (garbanzos)
1 small bunch of parsley, finely chopped or
    small sprigs of oregano/marjoram, to serve
salt and freshly ground black pepper

The Moorish flavours in this recipe could equally be found in Andalusia or north African cooking. Saffron, even in tiny quantities, can sometimes dominate ingredients, just as well then, given its price tag, that just a pinch is necessary to permeate a dish, lending an earthy, sweet flavour that offers a remarkable match for the lamb and the chickpeas in this dish. Spain is the origin of some of my favourite jarred chickpeas – plump, soft and extremely flavoursome – and depending on the juice in the jar of chickpeas, you can choose to drain your chickpeas, or do as I do with the jarred sort, up-ending the contents of the jar into the pan, then taking this pleasantly salted liquid in mind when it comes to seasoning the dish and just how much water you add to the pan to cook. The raisins in this dish offer a pleasing and sweet burst, I say optional, but very much recommend you add them.

1. In a bowl, mix the lamb with half the ground spices, 1 tablespoon of the olive oil, a squeeze of lemon juice, 1 garlic clove and salt and pepper. Leave to marinate, covered, in the fridge ideally for a minimum of 1 hour, although the longer, the better. Thread onto 4–5 skewers (don't overcrowd the skewers).

2. In a wide frying pan over a medium heat, sauté the lamb skewers for 4–5 minutes on each side until lightly coloured and cooked to your liking. Transfer to a plate and keep warm.

3. Add the remaining olive oil, the onion and raisins, if using, and cook with a pinch of salt for 10 minutes until the onion has softened and the raisins are plump.

4. Add the remaining garlic, the saffron, tomato purée and the remaining ground spices and cook for 30 seconds until aromatic.

5. Add the spinach and the chickpeas, stir to coat with the spices and add about 100ml (3½fl oz) of water. Cook until the spinach is wilted and the chickpeas are heated through. Season to taste with salt and pepper and add the lamb skewers back to the pan with a big squeeze of lemon juice to warm through.

6. Serve with a sprinkling of parsley or oregano/marjoram.

Creamy Mascarpone Butter Beans with Sausage and Gremolata

Serves 4

4 large good-quality pork sausages, skins removed and meat squeezed out
2 tbsp olive oil
3 garlic cloves, 2 thinly sliced, 1 roughly chopped
1 x 400g (14oz) can chopped tomatoes or polpa (finely chopped tomatoes)
1 small bunch of parsley, roughly chopped
2 strips of unwaxed lemon zest, pith removed
150g (5½oz) mascarpone
¼–½ nutmeg, freshly grated
approx. 750g (1lb 10oz) drained cooked or canned butter (lima) beans
pinch of chilli flakes (optional), plus more to serve
salt and freshly ground black pepper

To serve

4 thick slices of bread, toasted and drizzled with extra virgin olive oil
Parmesan, shaved or grated

I'm a big fan of using good-quality sausages, removed from their casings, to use in a base for bean (also pasta) recipes. Well-seasoned, they bring an easy, instant flavour boost to a dish and don't tend to cost all that much. As ingredients go, I find a little goes a long way, which, if you do eat meat, is a good maxim for using less and buying the best quality your budget can stretch to. One sausage per person is ample to flavour the beans and enough to feed four people, for example. If you want to keep this recipe meat-free, omit the sausages; I might be tempted to sauté some mushrooms in with the garlic to add extra oomph to the beans. Mascarpone makes these beans extra rich and creamy, and the gremolata is a fine accompaniment; using it in the beans, on the toast and also on the beans to serve ensures everything sings.

1. Using wet hands, break up the sausages into small chunks.

2. In a large pan over a moderate heat, fry the sausage meat chunks in the olive oil for 5–8 minutes until cooked and beginning to caramelize. Then add the sliced garlic and cook for a further 1 minute until fragrant.

3. Stir in the tomatoes and lower the heat. Cook for 10 minutes until the sauce is thickened and rich.

4. Meanwhile, chop together the parsley, lemon zest and garlic until very finely chopped to make the gremolata. Put to one side.

5. Add the mascarpone and nutmeg to the tomato and sausages and mix well. Check the seasoning, adding salt and black pepper to taste.

6. Stir in the beans and half the gremolata. Top with the chilli flakes (if using), adding a splash of water to loosen, if required.

7. Top the toasted bread slices with the beans and sprinkle over the remaining gremolata, the shaved parmesan and extra chilli flakes.

Chicken, Chickpea and Aubergine Tagine

Serves 4–6

1 small bunch of coriander (cilantro), stalks reserved, leaves finely chopped
4 garlic cloves, finely chopped
1 preserved lemon, pips removed, skin and flesh finely chopped
4 tbsp olive oil
800g (1lb 12oz) skinless, boneless chicken (thigh is best), diced into 4–5cm (1½–2in) pieces
1 large aubergine (eggplant), cut into 1cm (½in) slices
2 onions, thinly sliced
2 carrots, thinly sliced
1 cinnamon stick
3 tbsp butter
1 tsp ground cumin
1 tsp ground turmeric
1 tsp ground coriander
1 tsp ground ginger
1 tsp ras el hanout spice blend (optional)
3 ripe tomatoes or 1 x 400g (14oz) can plum tomatoes, roughly chopped
100g (3½oz) dried dates, pitted and roughly chopped
juice of ½ lemon
approx. 500g (1lb 2oz) drained cooked or canned chickpeas (garbanzos)
2 tbsp toasted flaked almonds
salt and freshly ground black pepper

To serve
couscous, cooked as per the packet instructions
harissa paste

Like pulses and legumes, aubergines are great at soaking up flavours, like in this tagine. Pre-frying the aubergine before adding the chickpeas helps to make the aubergine extra silky, and a great canvas for flavour. The trick to a good tagine lies in the ability of the cook to balance the flavours between the richness of the butter and the fried aubergine and the zip of the preserved lemon and lemon juice, the sweetness of the dried fruit, the earthy nutty flavours of the chickpeas, along with the aromatic spices and the heat from harissa. Taste, taste, taste as you cook this tagine, layering flavours, lending complexity.

1. In a blender, combine the coriander stalks with half the garlic, half the preserved lemon and 2 tablespoons of the olive oil and blend to a coarse purée.

2. Mix the purée into the chicken and leave to marinate, covered, in the fridge ideally for a minimum of 1 hour, although the longer, the better. Remove the chicken from the fridge about 20 minutes before you plan to cook it.

3. In a deep pan over a moderate heat, cook the aubergine slices in the remaining olive oil in batches for 2–3 minutes on each side until golden brown. Transfer the cooked slices to a plate and put to one side.

4. Wipe out the pan and, over a medium heat, add the butter, then add the onions, carrots and cinnamon stick with ½ teaspoon of salt and cook for 5 minutes until the onions have softened. Add the remaining garlic and the ground spices and cook for 30 seconds until aromatic, then stir in the tomatoes and dates and mix well.

5. Arrange the chicken and aubergine slices on top, add the remaining preserved lemon and lemon juice, then pour over 400ml (14fl oz) of water.

6. Bring to the boil, then lower the heat, cover and simmer very gently for about 35 minutes until the chicken is tender and cooked through and the aubergine is softened.

7. Add the chickpeas and chopped coriander leaves, season to taste with salt and pepper and warm through for 15 minutes. Remove from the heat and allow to rest for 5 minutes before sprinkling with the almonds and serving with couscous and harissa.

Chickpea and Tomato Bulgur Pilaf

Serves 4

300g (10½oz) coarse bulgur wheat
1 large onion, finely diced
50g (1¾oz) butter or olive oil
2 garlic cloves, finely chopped
4 Turkish green peppers or use 1 green (bell)
   pepper, deseeded and cut into large strips
2 tbsp Turkish pepper paste or 3 tsp tomato
   purée (paste) mixed with 3 tsp unsmoked
   sweet paprika
1 tsp ground cumin
½ tsp ground allspice
1 x 400g (14oz) can chopped tomatoes
approx. 750g (1lb 10oz) drained cooked or
   canned chickpeas (garbanzos)
salt and freshly ground black pepper

To serve
150g (5½oz) natural yogurt, seasoned with salt
chilli flakes (optional)
1 small bunch of mint, dill or parsley,
   roughly chopped

Bulgur brings a unique edge to pilafs, and I think this comes down to its wholegrain qualities, that is to say, a pleasingly chewy texture and nutty flavour. Add to the fact bulgur is easy to prepare and quicker to cook than rice, it is a go-to ingredient in my storecupboard along with a whole library of both dried and canned beans and pulses. You can use red, yellow or orange peppers for this recipe, but I recommend you use green peppers here as they are a good foil for the sweet onions and earthy chickpeas with a gentle, grassy bitterness.

1. Soak the bulgur in water for 10 minutes, then drain well.

2. While the bulgur is soaking, in a large pan over a moderate heat, cook the onion in the butter for 10 minutes until soft. Add the garlic and the green pepper strips and cook for 1 minute. Stir in the pepper paste, ground spices, ½ teaspoon of salt and the tomatoes and cook for 10 minutes to thicken.

3. Add the drained bulgur wheat and 400ml (14fl oz) of water and bring to the boil. Then sprinkle over the chickpeas, cover and simmer gently over a low heat for 15–20 minutes until the bulgur is tender and the water has been absorbed. Check the seasoning, adding salt and pepper to taste.

4. Serve the pilaf topped with yogurt and chilli flakes (if using) and sprinkled with the herbs.

Green Lentils and Leeks with Dragoncello Sauce

Serves 4

4 large leeks, trimmed and cut into 6cm (2½in)
   lengths and washed well

2 bay leaves

1 small bunch of tarragon, leaves picked,
   stalks reserved

juice of ½ unwaxed lemon, 3 strips of the zest
   reserved with the pith removed

6 garlic cloves, 5 peeled and halved,
   1 thinly sliced

80ml (2½fl oz) olive oil

1 tbsp white wine or cider vinegar

1 small slice of stale bread, crusts removed
   and ripped into small pieces

3 canned/jarred anchovies in oil, drained
   (optional if you want it to be vegan)

1 tsp capers

pickled egg, grated (optional – see
   introduction)

approx. 250g (9oz) drained cooked or canned
   green speckled or Puy lentils

salt and freshly ground black pepper

Lentils and leeks are a wonderful match. Dragoncello sauce is made with tarragon (dragoncello), and quite apart from having such an evocative name, is a gorgeous Italian sauce made with vinegar, anchovies, capers, day-old bread and olive oil. The vinegar in the dragoncello used to dress the just-cooked, warm lentils is alchemy. You could add a finely grated hard-boiled egg to the sauce if you like, or even just grate one all over the finished dish, but you would have to then have a quick word with yourself about using just one pan and be at peace with some extra washing up, or – good hack here – use a shop-bought pickled egg, grated in a flash. This is a great side dish, or serve it as a light lunch.

1. In a casserole over a medium heat, cook the leeks, bay leaves, 3 tarragon stalks, the lemon zest strips and halved garlic in half the olive oil with a big pinch of salt for 5 minutes, turning often. Turn the heat down to low, cover and cook the leeks for about 5 minutes until they are tender, then stir through the vinegar.

2. Meanwhile, place the bread in a bowl and cover with water.

3. Finely chop the tarragon leaves, sliced garlic, anchovies (if using) and capers and place in a bowl. Squeeze the excess water out of the bread, finely chop and add to the bowl, then stir in the remaining olive oil, the lemon juice and grated pickled egg (if using), until you achieve a nice loose consistency. Season to taste with salt and pepper.

4. Stir the lentils into the leeks and warm through. Serve topped with the sauce.

Turkish Borlotti Bean Pilaki

Serves 4

1 onion, finely chopped

1 large carrot, peeled and finely chopped

3 celery stalks, finely chopped

60ml (2fl oz) olive oil

6 garlic cloves, finely chopped

500g (1lb 2oz) potatoes, peeled and diced

2 tbsp Turkish pepper paste or use 3 tsp tomato purée (paste) mixed with 3 tsp unsmoked sweet paprika

200g (7oz) chopped tomatoes, fresh or canned

1–2 tsp Turkish chilli flakes, to taste, plus more to serve

2 tsp dried oregano

3 bay leaves

approx. 500g (1lb 2oz) drained cooked or canned borlotti (cranberry) beans

juice of ½ unwaxed lemon, plus 4 thin slices from the remaining lemon

2 tbsp honey

1 small bunch of parsley, roughly chopped, reserving a big pinch to serve

salt and freshly ground black pepper

Pilaki is a Turkish dish made with beans cooked in a sauce along with some aromatics and often some carrot and potato for good measure. There are no hard and fast rules, but this recipe is a good guideline. Serve as a mezze garnished with good olive oil and thin slices of lemon. I am using borlotti beans for this recipe, their purple-hued and mottled skin always stops me in my tracks. You can, if available, use fresh borlotti beans in the late summer and early autumn, or use dried and cooked or jarred or canned. I'll leave this up to you. Turkish pepper paste is readily available online, or from Middle Eastern stores and even bigger supermarkets. If you can't track any down, tomato purée mixed through with some sweet unsmoked paprika will do a good enough job to ape it.

1. In a large pan over a moderate heat, cook the onion, carrot and celery in the olive oil for 10 minutes until soft, then stir in the garlic and cook for 30 seconds.

2. Add the potatoes and cook for 1 minute to coat, then add the pepper paste, tomatoes, chilli flakes, oregano, bay leaves and a generous amount of black pepper. Simmer for about 5 minutes until thickened.

3. Add enough water to cover the potato and cook for 10 minutes until the potato is tender.

4. Add the beans and mix well to coat the beans with the sauce, then top up with boiling water, if needed, to just cover the beans.

5. Cover and cook for 5 minutes until the beans are heated through and the sauce is rich and thick. Stir in the lemon juice, lemon slices and honey and season to taste with salt and more pepper, if necessary.

6. Stir through the chopped parsley, cover and allow to rest for 5 minutes before serving, topped with some more chilli flakes.

Punjabi Red Kidney Beans with Caramelized Onions

Serves 4

2 black cardamom pods, bruised
1 cinnamon stick
2 bay leaves
50g (1½oz) ghee or sunflower oil
2 large onions, thinly sliced
1 tbsp finely grated fresh ginger
4 garlic cloves, crushed to a paste
4 green chillies
1 tsp ground cumin
1 tsp ground coriander
pinch of ground cloves
½ tsp ground ginger
1 tsp ground turmeric
½–2 tsp chilli powder, to taste
200g (7oz) chopped tomatoes, fresh or canned
1 tbsp tomato purée (paste)
approx. 750g (1lb 10oz) drained cooked or
   canned red kidney beans
juice of 1 lemon
2 tsp dried fenugreek leaves (kasoori methi)
salt and freshly ground black pepper

To serve
1 small bunch of coriander (cilantro), roughly
   chopped
1–4 green chillies, thinly sliced (optional)
2 tsp amchoor
40g (1½oz) crispy fried onions

Another Punjabi recipe here called rajma, also known as rajmah, rāzmā or lal lobia. The Punjab region is located in the northwest of the Indian subcontinent and it is also the most populous province of Pakistan. Straddling both India and Pakistan, the region's cuisine is a rich and culturally interesting one. I have not visited this particular region in India (though I have many others), but in the research for bean recipes to feature in this cookbook, this one stood out, and to my mind, anywhere that takes beans and showcases them to such dazzling effect as here in this recipe, is a cuisine that I very much admire. Onions, cooked down until soft and melting are also crucial here, absorbing the flavours of the sauce. Serving suggestions are yet more onions, either crispy fried onions (and the store-bought version are perfectly acceptable), or fresh onions, thinly sliced and dressed with a squeeze of lemon juice and a big pinch of salt. Typically this dish would be served with rice.

1. In a large saucepan over a moderate heat, cook the cardamom, cinnamon and bay leaves in the ghee for 2–3 minutes until fragrant.

2. Add the onions and a big pinch of salt and cook for 10–15 minutes until the onions are very soft and golden brown.

3. Add the ginger, garlic and whole green chillies and cook for 1 minute until fragrant, then stir in the ground cumin, coriander, cloves, ginger, turmeric and chilli powder and fry for 30 seconds.

4. Add the chopped tomatoes and tomato purée and cook for 5 minutes until thickened.

5. Add the kidney beans and 300ml (10fl oz) of water and simmer for 15–20 minutes until rich and thick, adding salt and pepper to taste and a splash more water, if required.

6. Squeeze the lemon juice over and stir the dried fenugreek leaves into the kidney beans, then scatter over the coriander, green chilli slices (if using), amchoor and crispy onions to serve.

Chicken with 40 Garlic Cloves and Butter Beans

Serves 4

4 large chicken thighs, bone in, skin on

1 tbsp Dijon mustard

40 garlic cloves (approx. 3–4 heads), unpeeled

2 tbsp extra virgin olive oil

3 bay leaves

3 thyme sprigs

300ml (10fl oz) hot chicken stock or water

3 tbsp dry white wine or dry sherry

750g (1lb 10oz) drained cooked or canned butter (lima) or cannellini beans

1 small bunch of parsley, roughly chopped

2 tbsp toasted almonds, roughly chopped

salt and freshly ground black pepper

In the wake of so many recipes for 40-cloves-of-garlic chicken, from many food writers, myself in a previous book included, the question must be asked, can it ever be bettered? And the answer is, yes it can, just add butter beans! The butter beans soak in the chicken and garlic juices, turning sensational. The quantity of garlic is not foolhardy, do take it seriously – as the garlic cooks it becomes sweet and intensely savoury and very delicious. Eat the garlic by squeezing the sweet soft flesh out of the bronzed skins, almost mashing it into the beans and liquid as you come across them. The toasted almonds thicken the juices and complement the beans and chicken immeasurably.

1. Season the chicken thighs with salt and pepper and coat with the mustard.

2. Place in an ovenproof dish over a moderate heat with the garlic and olive oil and brown for about 5 minutes, until lightly coloured. Add the bay leaves, thyme, stock and wine, bring to the boil, then turn the heat to low, cover and cook for 30 minutes, until just about cooked, then season the juices with salt and pepper to taste.

3. Add the beans, some of the parsley and almonds to the dish and give it a shake to coat, then warm through for 5 minutes until the chicken is cooked through and lightly coloured and the beans are piping hot. Add the remaining parsley and serve.

Black Bean and Carrot Burgers

Serves 4

approx. 250g (9oz) drained cooked or canned black beans or kidney beans
½ tsp chipotle powder or smoked paprika
1 tsp ground cumin
1 tsp dried oregano
1 tsp miso paste (any colour), or soy sauce
300g (10½oz) carrots, grated
½ bunch of spring onions (scallions), finely chopped
1 tbsp Dijon mustard
30g (1oz) ground almonds
70g (2½oz) dried breadcrumbs
30g (1oz) finely grated parmesan or cheddar cheese (optional)
sunflower or olive oil, for frying
salt and freshly ground black pepper

To serve

4 burger buns, halved
1 avocado, peeled, stoned and thinly sliced
2 large gherkins, thinly sliced
2 large pickled beetroots, thinly sliced
2 medium tomatoes, thinly sliced
1 small red onion, very thinly sliced
1 soft lettuce, leaves separated
mayonnaise (optional)
hot sauce (optional)

Beans (and black beans are my favourite here) make an excellent base for a plant-based burger. I like black beans as their colour works well, they have a deep savoury flavour and their soft skins break down nicely, but please, and by all means, you can choose any bean you prefer. For these burgers to hold nicely, I like to use a mixture of ground nuts, and with them, some healthy fats, also, some breadcrumbs for ballast. Enjoy in a bun with soft lettuce, avocado, some sliced gherkins and pickled beetroot for the win, very thinly sliced tomato and red onion and bottled condiments of your choice, though my hunch would always be hot sauce, and the hotter the better in a bean burger.

1. Blend or mash the beans to a rough purée with the chipotle powder, cumin, oregano and miso.

2. In a bowl, mix in the grated carrots, spring onions, mustard, ground almonds, breadcrumbs, grated cheese (if using) and seasoning to taste. Use your hands to work the mix together until cohesive and easily shaped.

3. Shape the mix into four burgers about 2cm (¾in) thick and place on a tray or plate. Put them in the fridge to firm up for an hour or so.

4. Heat a large non-stick frying pan with enough oil to cover the surface and fry the burgers over a moderate heat for 2–3 minutes on each side until crisp.

5. Remove from the heat and serve immediately inside the burger buns with the avocado, gherkin, pickled beetroot, tomato, red onion, lettuce and with mayonnaise and/or hot sauce (if using).

Chickpea Fritters
with Yogurt and Feta

Serves 4

approx. 250g (9oz) drained cooked or canned
  chickpeas (garbanzos)
1 tsp ground turmeric
100g (3½oz) natural yogurt, plus extra to serve
3 eggs
100g (3½oz) feta, roughly crumbled, plus
  another 100g (3½oz) to serve
2 tbsp sesame seeds
1 tsp nigella seeds
1 small bunch of coriander (cilantro),
  roughly chopped
100g (3½oz) self-raising (self-rising) flour
vegetable or olive oil, for frying
salt and freshly ground black pepper

To serve
1–2 fresh green chillies, thinly sliced
hot sauce (optional)

Try using extra plump soft chickpeas for this recipe, the sort you've cooked yourself or use those especially chubby ones from a jar – you want the chickpeas to partially break down, meaning each mouthful is slightly different in composition. These fritters are very user-friendly as the mixture not only keeps well in the fridge for a few hours and is easy to prepare ahead, but is also extremely versatile when it comes to what to serve the fritters with – a whole host of fridge favourite condiments from ketchups, salsas, relishes, chutneys and mustards to creamy sauces such as mayonnaise and seasoned yogurt. The recipe affords a good amount of flexibility in the herbs, seeds and spices used, so do play around with different combinations once you have this version mastered. It is a lightning fast meal.

1. Roughly mash the chickpeas in a large bowl, leaving plenty whole or partially crushed. Stir through the turmeric, yogurt and eggs.

2. Stir through 100g (3½oz) of the crumbled feta, all the seeds and three-quarters of the coriander, then season to taste with salt and pepper. Finally, gently fold through the flour.

3. In a hot frying pan over a moderate heat, add a film of oil and fry heaped tablespoonfuls of the batter for about 2 minutes until the bottoms have firmed enough to flip over, then fry on the other side for another 2 minutes. When cooked, transfer to a warm plate and cover with a dish towel. Fry the fritters in small batches until all the mixture is used up.

4. Serve the fritters topped with the remaining crumbled feta, drizzled with yogurt and topped with the remaining coriander and the green chilli slices. Serve with hot sauce to accompany, if you like.

Falafel with Tahini Sauce

Serves 4

200g (7oz) dried chickpeas (garbanzos), soaked overnight in cold water
2 garlic cloves, crushed to a paste
1 bunch of spring onions (scallions), finely chopped
1 small bunch of coriander (cilantro), leaves picked and finely chopped
1 large bunch of flat-leaf parsley, leaves picked and finely chopped
½ tsp baking powder
1 tsp ground coriander
1 tsp ground cumin
½ tsp salt
½ tsp freshly ground black pepper, or to taste
sunflower oil, for frying

To serve
3 tbsp tahini
150g (5½oz) natural yogurt
pinch of sumac
1 cucumber, peeled and finely chopped
2 medium tomatoes, finely chopped
1 Little Gem lettuce, thinly sliced
1 small bunch of mint, roughly chopped or smaller leaves
1 small red chilli, thinly sliced
1 lemon
4 pitta breads, toasted and split
chilli sauce (optional)
salt and freshly ground black pepper

There is something very, very good about a freshly fried falafel. They are a completely different entity to precooked and packaged falafel (pass the cardboard to chew on, please). Freshly fried, they are one of the most wholesome options in the cannon of deep-fried food! The raw chickpeas (you cannot use cooked chickpeas, the falafel will not hold), along with all the herbs and flavourings, give a fluffy, soft interior which works so well with the gnarled, crisp and golden exterior. You know the drill – fried off, stuff them in warm pitta breads, with tahini sauce, hot sauce, lemon juice and lots of chopped salad. To ensure all your falafel are as delicious as can be, fry off a little of the mixture first to check the seasoning, then adjust if needed. Don't overcrowd the pan and keep the oil at a steady temperature of 180°C (350°F). Used oil can be cooled, strained through a fine sieve and re-used up to three times.

1. Rinse the soaked chickpeas and drain well. Place in a food processor with the garlic, spring onions, herbs, baking powder, ground spices, salt and pepper and blend with a splash of water until you have a smooth green paste.

2. Heat a little sunflower oil in a medium high-sided saucepan over a moderate heat and fry 1 teaspoon of the mixture to check the seasoning. Adjust with more salt and pepper if necessary. Chill the rest of the mixture in the fridge for at least 30 minutes.

3. Meanwhile, blend or mix the tahini and yogurt and season to taste with salt and pepper. Drizzle with a little extra olive oil and sprinkle with pinch of sumac and put to one side.

4. In a bowl, mix the cucumber, tomatoes, lettuce, mint and red chilli with the juice of half the lemon and season to taste.

5. Heat about 15cm (6in) of oil in the same saucepan until very hot. If you have a digital thermometer, about 180°C (350°F) is best. Using one spoon to scoop and another to scrape, add the falafel mixture very carefully into the hot oil. (Alternatively you can use a falafel shaper.) It should bubble vigorously for 3–4 minutes, turning over until crisp and golden brown. Work in small batches of about 6 at a time, removing the falafel with a slotted spoon to a plate lined with greaseproof paper.

6. Serve with the tahini sauce, salad, toasted and split pittas and chilli sauce (if using), with the remaining lemon cut into wedges.

Lentil and Beef Meatballs

Serves 4

For the meatballs

500g (1lb 2oz) minced (ground) beef
150g (5½oz) ricotta
120g (4¼oz) drained cooked or canned
  green or speckled lentils
1 egg
50g (1¾oz) fine dried white breadcrumbs
20g (¾oz) parmesan or pecorino, finely grated,
  plus more to serve
4 sage leaves, very finely chopped
freshly grated nutmeg
olive oil, for frying
salt and freshly ground black pepper

For the tomato sauce

2 tbsp olive oil
3 garlic cloves, finely chopped
10 sage leaves
400g (14oz) tomato passata (strained
  tomatoes)
120g (4¼oz) drained cooked or canned
  green or speckled lentils
pinch of chilli flakes (optional), plus more
  to serve

Lentils give these meatballs a lovely flavour boost as well as helping them to be a bit more rounded nutritionally, not to mention stretching the quantity of meat bought with a less costly ingredient! Mixing the meatball mixture well is worth the effort, it helps to emulsify the ingredients, boosting texture and, importantly, succulence. You're looking for the mixture to be a bit sticky and springy but to hold together well. Resting the meatball mixture before shaping allows the mixture to fully hydrate so it's easier to shape and allows the salt to work on the proteins in the meat, improving the tenderness of the meatball when it cooks. More lentils in the sauce, because… why not!

1. For the meatballs, in a large bowl, mix the minced beef, ricotta, lentils, egg, breadcrumbs, cheese and sage and season generously with nutmeg, salt and pepper.

2. Knead the mixture for 5 minutes until it just begins to feel cohesive and a bit sticky. Allow to rest for at least 30 minutes in the fridge, although a couple of hours is good.

3. Wet your hands and roll the meatball mixture into little balls about the size of a ping-pong ball. Put the balls on a plate in the fridge to firm up for 30 minutes or more.

4. In a large frying pan over a moderate heat, fry the meatballs in a film of olive oil in a single layer, in batches if needed, for 5–8 minutes until browned, then place on a plate to the side.

5. In the same pan, add the 2 tablespoons of olive oil, the garlic and sage leaves and cook for 30 seconds until aromatic.

6. Add the passata and season with salt and pepper. Bring to the boil, then turn the heat down to a simmer and cook for 10 minutes until the tomato sauce has thickened. Stir through the lentils and chilli flakes (if using) and check the seasoning.

7. Add the meatballs to the top of the sauce to gently warm through, then serve the meatballs topped with a grating of parmesan and a few more chilli flakes (if using).

Caramelized Cabbage and Ancho Chillies with Bean Purée

Serves 4

3 dried ancho or pasilla chillies, destemmed, deseeded and thinly sliced

1 large firm hispi cabbage, quartered into wedges, or 2 small cabbages, cut in half

2 tbsp olive oil, plus more for rubbing and frying

approx. 250g (9oz) drained cooked or canned white beans

1 small bunch of coriander (cilantro), roughly chopped

2 garlic cloves, thinly sliced

1 tsp ground cumin

3 tbsp cider or white wine vinegar

salt and freshly ground black pepper

2 tbsp toasted pumpkin seeds, to serve

Caramelizing cabbages has been on trend for a number of years now, for good reason, as charring the leaves boosts texture and flavour and also tastes completely delicious. Pointed hispi cabbages especially enjoy this treatment as the loose-leafed structure of the cabbage allows for a range of textures and colouration. Once cooked, the wedges have a rustic beauty and can make an eye-catching side dish, more like a centrepiece. Serving the charred cabbage on a bean purée all spiked with chilli, cumin and garlic, the lot then showered with plenty of chopped coriander, is a winning combination.

1. Soak the chillies in boiling water for 3 minutes, then drain and discard the soaking liquid. Set to one side.

2. Rub the cabbage lightly with olive oil and season generously with salt, ensuring that all sides are well coated.

3. In a large frying pan over a moderate heat, fry the cabbage wedges in a film of olive oil for 10–12 minutes, turning often enough until nicely charred and wilted.

4. While the cabbage is cooking, blend the beans with half the coriander, half the garlic and the cumin. Then stir through the 2 tablespoons of olive oil, half the vinegar and half the chillies, adding salt and pepper to taste. Put to one side.

5. When the cabbage is tender, stir through the remaining garlic, sliced chillies and vinegar and toss to coat, then cook for 1 minute.

6. Spread the bean purée on a serving plate, arrange the cabbage over the top and then sprinkle with the pumpkin seeds and the remaining coriander.

Chorizo, Cider and White Beans

**Serves 4 as a
tapas or starter or
2 as a main meal**

2 tbsp olive oil

4–8 cooking chorizo (400g/14oz)

2 garlic cloves, finely chopped

2 bay leaves

250ml (9fl oz) dry cider

approx. 500g (1lb 2oz) drained cooked or
canned large white beans

1 small bunch of flat-leaf parsley, roughly
chopped

salt and freshly ground black pepper

4 thick slices of robust bread, toasted and
rubbed with raw garlic clove and olive oil

When I had my restaurant, this really simple Northern Spanish dish of chorizo cooked in cider was a bit of a mainstay on the menu and it was always a favourite with the customers. The cider and the chorizo create a deeply flavoured sauce that the beans can soak in, making the beans the true star of the show. The bay is important here in this short list of ingredients, bringing with it a warm, herbal note. Serve this as a tapas dish in combination with other small dishes, though I would happily serve this as is with a good crusty bread to mop up the juices.

1. Heat the olive oil in a frying pan over a moderate heat, add the chorizo and cook over a low heat for about 5 minutes until the chorizo is golden and releases its fat into the pan.

2. Add the garlic and bay leaves and fry for about 1 minute until fragrant, then pour in the cider and cook for 5–8 minutes over a moderate heat until thick and syrupy.

3. Stir through the beans and parsley and season to taste with salt and pepper.

4. Serve the chorizo and beans with the toasted bread.

Chickpea, Prawn and Cabbage Egg Fried Rice

Serves 4

4 large eggs

2 tbsp soy sauce

1 tsp fish sauce or extra soy sauce

4 tbsp vegetable or sunflower oil

1 tbsp finely grated fresh ginger

2 garlic cloves, thinly sliced

1 small hispi cabbage, core removed and cut into thin wedges or shredded

250g (9oz) peeled and deveined medium raw prawns (shrimp), or firm tofu, diced

1 bunch of spring onions (scallions), thinly sliced

1 tsp sesame oil

500g (1lb 2oz) cooked rice (short-grain brown is good), cooled

approx. 250g (9oz) drained cooked or canned chickpeas (garbanzos)

2 tsp sesame seeds, toasted

fresh red chilli, thinly sliced, to serve

Adding chickpeas to a stir-fry isn't conventional, but they work brilliantly, adding texture and extra nutritional boost. The secret to egg-fried rice is to have the cooked rice cool or cold, which helps keep the grains separate when frying. For ultra swift assembly, ensure you've got everything to hand, chopped or sliced and good to go. I personally really like the nutty flavour of brown rice in a stir-fry. A whole grain with more fibre and micronutrients than white rice, brown rice is the nutritionally superior and tastier option here. I also think short-grain brown rice works especially well in a stir-fry, with a pleasingly chewy texture, holding its own, as it does, among all the other ingredients.

1. In a small bowl, beat the eggs together with the soy sauce and fish sauce.

2. Heat 1 tablespoon of the oil in a wok or a large non-stick frying pan over a moderate-high heat. Add the ginger and garlic and fry for about 30 seconds until fragrant, then stir in the cabbage and stir-fry for 2 minutes until slightly wilted. Remove to a plate and put to one side.

3. Put the wok back on the heat and add 1 more tablespoon of oil. Add the prawns and spring onions and fry over a moderate heat for 2–3 minutes until the prawns are cooked through. Set aside the prawns and spring onions along with the cabbage on the plate.

4. Add the remaining vegetable oil, along with the sesame oil, to the wok. Heat the oil until very hot and add the cooled rice. Stir-fry the rice, ensuring all the grains get coated in the hot oil.

5. Add the beaten eggs and the chickpeas to the rice and continue to fry until all the egg is absorbed by the rice. Stir vigorously and fry for about 3 minutes, or until some of the rice begins to caramelize.

6. Return the cabbage and prawn mixture to the wok. Toss the rice, prawns and cabbage together until everything is heated through.

7. Serve immediately with the sesame seeds and chilli sprinkled on top.

White Bean and Lemon Fishcakes

Serves 4

approx. 250g (9oz) drained cooked or canned white beans

300g (10½oz) hot-smoked salmon, trout or mackerel, skin and bones removed, and flaked

1 tbsp Dijon mustard

2 tbsp mayonnaise, plus more to serve

1 unwaxed lemon, zest finely grated and the lemon thinly sliced

1 large egg, beaten

40g (1½oz) fine fresh breadcrumbs, plus 3 tbsp to coat the fishcakes

1 small bunch of chives or parsley, finely chopped

olive oil, for frying

salt and freshly ground black pepper

To serve

brown or white seeded rolls, to serve

soft lettuce leaves, washed and separated, to serve

Replacing the more traditional mashed potatoes with mashed white beans in this recipe isn't just a sneaky twist but makes this an especially speedy recipe, one perfect for a midweek one-pan dinner. The fishcakes can be served like you might have a burger in a roll as suggested below, but equally, they are great served alongside a chopped salad made with some tomatoes, spring onions, any soft herb, lemon juice and olive oil and, go for it, maybe even some more white beans! I was taught the hack of adding mayonnaise to fishcakes back in the early days of being a chef – it lends an extra creaminess and moisture to the fishcakes and helps them to bind. Frying thin slices of lemon until softly caramelized is one of my favourite ways to use all of the lemon – zest in the fishcakes and fried whole slices, all chewy and lemony, as the garnish. So good!

1. Mash or pulse the beans in a small food processor into a smoothish mash.

2. Stir the mustard, mayonnaise, lemon zest, egg and a pinch of salt into the mashed bean mixture. Gently fold in the flaked fish with the breadcrumbs and the herbs until everything is evenly distributed and holding together nicely. If you think the mix is too wet, add another tablespoon of breadcrumbs. Season to taste with salt and pepper.

3. Scoop a quarter of the mixture and roll it between your palms to form a ball. Pat the ball into a flat cake about 3cm (1¼in) thick, then put to one side on a plate and continue with the remaining mix. Sprinkle the fishcakes on both sides with the additional 3 tablespoons of breadcrumbs.

4. In a large frying pan, over a medium heat, pour in a thin film of olive oil to heat, and add the fishcakes once the oil is shimmering. Don't overcrowd the pan and cook in batches if required. Fry for about 2 minutes on each side until they have turned golden brown with a good crust. Place on a plate lined with kitchen paper to soak up excess fat and continue to fry the remaining fishcakes if cooking in batches. Fry the lemon slices until softly caramelized.

5. To serve, add the fishcakes to the bread rolls with soft lettuce and some extra mayonnaise, and top with the fried lemon slices.

Butter Bean, Goat's Cheese and Chard Frittata

Serves 4

approx. 250g (9oz) drained cooked or canned
 butter (lima) beans
80ml (2¾fl oz) milk
7 eggs, beaten
2 leeks, trimmed, washed and thinly sliced
6 large stalks of chard, stems removed and
 thinly sliced, leaves thinly sliced
3 tbsp olive oil
1 small bunch of basil, leaves picked
150g (5½oz) goat's cheese log, thinly sliced
30g (1oz) parmesan, finely grated, plus more
 to serve
salt and freshly ground black pepper

Chard, and other wilted dark green leaves, like spinach and cavolo nero, work extremely well here with the white beans and the caramelized leeks all cooked into a frittata. I've added some ricotta and plenty of parmesan to the eggs to create a classic one-pan dish – superb to eat just out of the oven, at room temperature or even cooled and cut into wedges for a picnic or packed lunch. If chard isn't available, substitute with spinach or similar, or just add more leeks, this is a fail-safe recipe – where would we be without frittata in the world?

1. Preheat the oven to 200°C/180°C fan/400°F/Gas 6.

2. Blend half the beans with the milk and eggs, season to taste with salt and pepper and put to one side.

3. In a non-stick, ovenproof frying pan over a medium heat, fry the leeks and chard stalks in the olive oil for 8–10 minutes until the leeks are tender and sweet. Add the chard leaves, cover and cook for 3–5 minutes, stirring every now and then until the leaves have softened and wilted down.

4. Add the remaining whole beans and half the basil leaves to the pan and mix to combine.

5. Pour the egg mixture over the leek mixture in the hot pan. Turn down the heat, dot with the goat's cheese slices on top and sprinkle with the parmesan and a grind of pepper. Take the pan off the heat and bake in the hot oven for 8–12 minutes, or until firm to the touch and golden brown on top.

6. Remove from the oven and allow to rest for 5 minutes before sliding out onto a chopping board or large plate. Serve while still warm, or cold, topped with a little more parmesan and the remaining basil leaves.

Chickpea Jalfrezi

Serves 4

approx. 750g (1lb 10oz) drained cooked or
  canned chickpeas (garbanzos)
½ tsp chilli flakes or chilli powder
juice of 1 lemon
2 red onions, thinly sliced
1 tbsp garam masala
½ tsp ground turmeric
4 garlic cloves, finely chopped
1 tbsp finely grated fresh ginger
4 tbsp ghee or sunflower oil
2 tsp mustard seeds
2 tsp cumin seeds
2 tbsp tomato purée (paste)
2 (bell) peppers (any colour), deseeded
  and sliced
3 medium ripe tomatoes, each cut into
  6 wedges
salt and freshly ground black pepper

To serve
sliced green chillies (optional)
naan or cooked rice
lemon wedges

This type of restaurant-style curry has less sauce than some, verging on a stir-fry or dry-fry curry method. Using the blended onion, combined with the spices, is crucial in this curry method. Jalfrezi should have a good degree of sourness from the hit of lemon juice along with lots of juicy, fresh tomatoes. Also key to this curry preparation is first cooking the seeds in the oil, then adding the spiced onion paste to cook down and, finally, to finish, more garam masala to really send the scent of the spices reeling. The chickpeas are a welcome canvas for all those flavours.

1. Mix the chickpeas together with the chilli flakes, half the lemon juice and a big pinch of salt and put to one side.

2. Using a blender, blend a quarter of the onions, half the garam masala, the turmeric, garlic, ginger and remaining lemon juice to a paste.

3. Heat the ghee in a large frying pan or wok over a moderate-high heat. Add the mustard and cumin seeds and fry for 30 or so seconds until they begin to sizzle. Add the onion purée and tomato purée and cook for 5–8 minutes until the liquid has cooked away and the paste is beginning to stick without burning.

4. Add the remaining onions and the peppers and stir fry for 5–7 minutes, or until they are softened, but still have some texture, and the liquid has concentrated and is thickened.

5. Add the tomatoes and chickpeas mixture and stir-fry for 2 minutes. Add a tiny splash of water if the mixture is getting too dry and beginning to catch. Check the dish for seasoning, adjusting with more salt and pepper, if you like.

6. Sprinkle over the sliced green chillies (if using) and the remaining garam masala. Serve straight away with naan or cooked rice.

Fried Sprouts with Lentils and Walnuts

Serves 4

400g (14oz) Brussels sprouts, trimmed
2 thyme sprigs, leaves picked
2 dried juniper berries, crushed and
    finely chopped
4 tbsp olive oil
2 garlic cloves, finely chopped
3 tbsp cider or white wine vinegar
2 tsp Dijon mustard
1 tbsp Marmite
finely grated zest of 1 unwaxed orange
45g (1½oz) butter
approx. 250g (9oz) drained cooked or canned
    dark green or speckled lentils
50g (1¾oz) lightly toasted walnuts, roughly
    chopped
1 small bunch of mint, leaves picked and
    roughly chopped
salt and freshly ground black pepper

I'm a big fan of roasting or sautéing sprouts until nicely coloured but still with a bit of bite – the caramelizing process enhances the natural sweetness in the sprouts. Lentils work really well here with the sprouts, dressed warm with some zippy vinegar. The juniper, orange zest and thyme is a delicious combination – add mustard, Marmite and walnuts and you have lentils as you've never had them before! Great as a side dish (think Christmas revamp for sprouts!) or as a light lunch.

1. Toss the sprouts with the thyme, juniper berries and 2 tablespoons of the olive oil and season with salt and pepper.

2. In a large frying pan over a moderate-high heat, fry the sprouts mixture in the remaining olive oil for 8–10 minutes until they are softened and beginning to colour. Do this in batches if required.

3. Add the garlic and cook for 30 seconds. Stir in the vinegar, mustard, Marmite, orange zest and butter and stir well to coat the sprouts and concentrate the vinegar.

4. Stir through the lentils, season to taste with salt and pepper and warm through. Serve topped with the walnuts and mint.

Assassin's Spaghetti

Serves 4

3 garlic cloves, thinly sliced

1–2 tsp chilli flakes, or more to taste,
   go for it!

60ml (2fl oz) olive oil

400g (14oz) thin spaghetti or spaghettini

1 tbsp tomato purée (paste)

500g (1lb 2oz) passata (strained tomatoes)

approx. 250g (9oz) drained cooked or canned
   fava beans or use chickpeas (garbanzos)

salt and freshly ground black pepper

This recipe had to go in the book, after all it is very much a one-pan pasta dish. It is said to originate from Puglia in southern Italy and so-called because the dish must be made with so much chilli it could almost kill you. I first saw this recipe watching Stanley Tucci's TV programme *Searching Italy*; the pasta is cooked in a risotto method – dry, uncooked pasta in a pan with passata and water added to cook the pasta, and ideally, as the liquids are absorbed, the pasta then sticks and almost burns in the pan. You want the pasta scorched and for the chilli to be first and foremost. I've taken the liberty of adding some fava beans to my spaghetti, and they are commonly used in this part of Italy; here they work brilliantly with the pasta – no cheese necessary – this is all about the chilli!

1. In a large non-stick or cast-iron frying pan (ideally wide enough to hold the spaghetti), cook the garlic and chilli flakes in the olive oil over a medium heat for 1–2 minutes, stirring until the garlic is just beginning to colour and the chilli sizzles nicely.

2. Meanwhile, boil the kettle, keep hot and near to hand.

3. Carefully place the spaghetti into the pan and mix to coat in the garlic and chilli oil. (The spaghetti should fit lengthways, but you can break to fit if needed.) Add the tomato purée and passata and fork through the pasta strands with the passata – you want the pasta evenly coated in the passata and oil. Season well with salt and pepper. Allow the pasta to cook for around 5 minutes, frying quite hard so the passata and pasta sizzles and the pasta sticks to the bottom of the pan. Carefully dislodge the spaghetti strands as they begin to stick, then pour over 200ml (7fl oz) of the boiled water. Continue cooking, trying to get the pasta to stick to the bottom of the pan as the liquid evaporates, then add another 200ml (7fl oz) of boiled water, repeating the process.

4. Keep adding boiling water, 200ml (7fl oz) at a time, each time letting the pasta absorb the liquid; try to keep the pasta in an even layer as it cooks in the pan – it should sizzle and crackle as it catches. Ideally, after the final addition of liquid, you then let the pasta catch, almost scorching in the pan as it sticks to get that nice texture when it is served. Add the fava beans and gently stir in to coat. Check a piece of pasta to see if it's ready, it should be al dente. (If your pasta is still on the firmer side, add a splash more water and continue to cook until it is ready.) Serve immediately.

BAKED
& ROASTED

Borlotti Bean and Beef Meatloaf

Serves 4

approx. 500g (1lb 2oz) drained cooked or
  canned borlotti (cranberry), black or red
  kidney beans
50ml (1¾fl oz) milk
4 tbsp olive oil
1 large egg
30g (1oz) fine dried breadcrumbs
500g (1lb 2oz) minced (ground) beef
½ tsp freshly ground black pepper
1 tsp ground fennel seeds
¼ tsp ground nutmeg
½ tsp chilli flakes
2 garlic cloves, crushed
40g (1½oz) parmesan, coarsely grated, plus
  more to serve
1 small bunch of parsley or oregano,
  roughly chopped
3 sage or thyme sprigs, leaves picked and
  finely chopped
3 carrots, coarsely grated
1 bunch of spring onions (scallions), finely
  chopped
2 bay leaves
3 celery stalks, finely chopped
400g (14oz) passata (strained tomatoes)
  or canned tomato pulp
salt

A good meatloaf will resonate with those of you fond of old-school comfort food, here with a twist to just add beans. I've gone broadly Italian, even Tuscan, here with the flavours used, but as ever, once you have the recipe down pat, by all means then let loose with alternative flavours such as adding chilli, diced chorizo and rosemary, BBQ seasoning flavours and so on – you get the picture. I've doubled up the beans in this recipe by adding them to the sauce too, so all in all, this is a great bean-centred recipe, with the quantity of meat bought stretching above and beyond. I find it makes for excellent leftovers too, used as a filling for a ciabatta roll or baguette; this makes for a killer panini or sandwich filling the next day.

1. Preheat the oven to 190°C/170°C fan/375°F/Gas 5.

2. In a blender, blend half the beans with the milk, 2 tablespoons of the olive oil and the egg, then stir through the breadcrumbs.

3. Mix this mixture into the minced beef along with the salt, pepper, ground fennel, nutmeg, chilli flakes, garlic and cheese. Add half of each of the chopped herbs, carrots and spring onions and mix to combine thoroughly. Shape into a log and top with the bay leaves, then put to one side.

4. In a large ovenproof, flameproof dish, over a moderate heat, cook the celery and the remaining carrots and spring onions in the remaining olive oil, with a pinch of salt, for 5 minutes to soften.

5. Stir through the passata and 100ml (3½fl oz) water and place the meatloaf on top.

6. Bake in the oven for 1 hour–1 hour 15 minutes until the meatloaf is cooked through and the sauce is rich and thick. Stir the remaining beans into the sauce and place back in the oven for 5 minutes for the beans to warm through.

7. Allow to rest for 5 minutes, remove the bay leaves and slice the meatloaf, then serve topped with the remaining chopped herbs and a little more grated parmesan.

Black Bean Chilli with Cornbread

Serves 4

1 large onion, finely diced

2 celery stalks, finely diced

1 green (bell) pepper, deseeded and
   finely chopped

2 carrots, coarsely grated

2–3 garlic cloves, finely chopped

4 tbsp olive oil

1 tbsp red wine vinegar

¼ tsp ground cinnamon

1 tsp smoked paprika, hot or sweet,
   depending on taste

1 tsp cumin seeds, toasted and ground

1–3 tsp chipotle chilli paste, to taste

1 tsp cocoa powder

½ tsp dried oregano

1 x 400g (14oz) can chopped tomatoes

approx. 500g (1lb 2oz) drained cooked or
   canned black or red kidney beans

salt and freshly ground black pepper

For the cornbread topping

150g (5½oz) coarse polenta (cornmeal)

100g (3½oz) self-raising (self-rising) flour

1 tsp baking powder

250ml (9fl oz) buttermilk or thin plain yogurt

1 tbsp runny honey, plus more to brush

50g (1¾oz) melted butter or olive oil, plus more
   to brush

2 eggs, beaten

pinch of dried oregano, plus more to sprinkle

2 spring onions (scallions), thinly sliced

50g (1¾oz) cheddar, grated

To serve

sour cream

roughly chopped coriander (cilantro)

hot sauce (optional)

Cornbread is such a wonderful foil for the beans in this recipe. Using the cornbread as a topping for the beans is a good alternative to a traditional cobbler topping commonly made with flour and butter for lots of different stews and braises. Hot honey in with the cornbread mix and to lace the top with lots of melted butter is a revelation, which gives you a frankly stupendous-tasting cornbread to plough through to get to the richly spiced beans – as near a perfect mouthful as you can get. Have sour cream, chopped coriander and hot sauce at the ready to serve alongside.

1. Preheat the oven to 210°C/190°C fan/410°F/Gas 6½.

2. In a large, ovenproof frying pan or shallow casserole over a medium heat, cook the onion, celery, green pepper, carrots and garlic with the olive oil and ½ teaspoon of salt for 10 minutes, stirring a few times, until the vegetables are soft and golden.

3. Meanwhile, to make the cornbread, in a bowl, mix together the polenta, flour and baking powder, then stir in the buttermilk, honey, melted butter, eggs, oregano, spring onions and cheddar and a generous grinding of black pepper.

4. Stir the vinegar, ground spices, chipotle paste, cocoa powder, dried oregano and tomatoes into the veg and cook for 5 minutes until thickened. Stir in the beans and enough boiling water to give a thick soupy texture, then season to taste with salt and pepper.

5. Spoon the cornbread mixture over the surface of the beans, then bake for 20–25 minutes until the topping is firm to touch and golden and the beans are bubbling.

6. Remove from the oven, brush with a bit more butter and honey, and finish with a sprinkle of dried oregano. Serve with sour cream, chopped coriander and hot sauce (if using).

Roasted Broccoli and Leeks with Lentils and Anchovies

Serves 4

300ml (10fl oz) double (heavy) cream

2 garlic cloves, finely chopped

finely grated zest of ½ unwaxed lemon

4 canned/jarred anchovies in oil, drained and finely chopped (optional)

approx. 250g (9oz) drained cooked or canned dark green or speckled lentils

3 medium leeks, washed, trimmed and sliced 3–4cm (1¼–1½in) thick

500g (1lb 2oz) sprouting broccoli, thick stalks trimmed

4 small shallots, thinly sliced

3 tbsp olive oil

30g (1oz) breadcrumbs

30g (1oz) parmesan, finely grated

salt and freshly ground black pepper

The slender stems of sprouting broccoli are one of those green vegetables that appreciate a number of different cooking methods – steaming, boiling and, in this case, roasting, with the stems and florets offering different textures as they cook, also intensifying in flavour during the cooking process. Add a sweet tangle of soft, cooked leeks with some lentils, dressed with cream, anchovies and quite a bit of garlic, before smothering the lot with some breadcrumbs to bake until bubbling and golden. This is a gratin to end all gratins. This recipe works well as a side dish but stands up as a centrepiece meal, in and of itself, very, very happily indeed, perhaps with a green salad and good bread to mop up.

1. Preheat the oven to 190°C/170°C fan/375°F/Gas 5.

2. In a bowl, mix the cream with the garlic, lemon zest and anchovies (if using) and season to taste with salt and pepper. Stir through the lentils and put to one side.

3. In a deep baking dish, toss the leeks, broccoli and shallots with the olive oil and season with salt and pepper. Roast the vegetables for 20–25 minutes until softened and beginning to colour in places.

4. Stir and pour over the cream mixture, then sprinkle over the breadcrumbs and return to the oven for 5–10 minutes until the topping is bubbling.

5. Serve sprinkled with the parmesan.

White Bean and Squash Gratin with Chestnuts and Hazelnuts

Serves 4

1kg (2lb 4oz) squash, sliced 1cm (½in) thick and deseeded (skin on if it's edible – look out for seasonal varieties such as crown prince, acorn or delicata)

1 red onion, thinly sliced

1 fennel bulb, trimmed and thinly sliced

3 tbsp extra virgin olive oil, plus more to drizzle

2 garlic cloves, finely chopped

2 rosemary or sage sprigs, leaves picked and finely chopped

approx. 500g (1lb 2oz) drained cooked or canned white beans

100g (3½oz) cooked (peeled) chestnuts, thinly sliced (optional)

150g (5½oz) cooked or frozen (and defrosted) whole leaf spinach

200ml (7fl oz) vegetable stock

30g (1oz) parmesan, finely grated

30g (1oz) breadcrumbs

30g (1oz) hazelnuts, roughy chopped

salt and freshly ground black pepper

freshly grated nutmeg, to serve

The combination here is an excellent one. The squash and white beans make a terrific canvas for the crunchy hazelnut topping. Choose a good squash or culinary pumpkin for this recipe; come the autumn, they are one of my favourite seasonal ingredients and we are spoilt for choice. Choose wisely and extensively from the assortment of squash and pumpkins on offer, it is one of life's great culinary adventures! This recipe is great as a side dish but will work just as well on its own. Use chard, cavolo nero or kale instead of the spinach, if you like.

1. Preheat the oven to 200°C/180°C fan/400°F/Gas 6.

2. In a deep baking dish, toss the squash, onion and fennel with the olive oil, garlic and rosemary and season with salt and pepper. Roast for 20–25 minutes until softened and beginning to colour.

3. Stir through the beans, chestnuts (if using), spinach and vegetable stock and return to the oven for 5 minutes, stirring once or twice until you have a slightly thickened stew consistency. Season to taste with salt and pepper.

4. Sprinkle over the parmesan, breadcrumbs and hazelnuts and drizzle with olive oil. Return the dish to the hot oven and bake for 15–20 minutes until the topping is crunchy and golden brown and the filling is bubbling.

5. Allow to rest for 5 minutes before serving topped with a grating of nutmeg.

Lentil and Mushroom Pie with Wholemeal Pastry

Serves 4

For the pastry

150g (5½oz) wholemeal (wholewheat) flour
150g (5½oz) plain (all-purpose) flour
150g (5½oz) chilled butter, diced
1 egg, beaten

For the filling

1 onion, finely chopped
1 leek, trimmed, washed and finely chopped
3 celery stalks, finely chopped
1 carrot, coarsely grated
3 tbsp olive oil
2 garlic cloves, finely chopped
2 thyme sprigs, leaves picked and
   finely chopped
400g (14oz) mushrooms, sliced
1 tbsp wholemeal (wholewheat) flour
1 tbsp tomato purée (paste)
1 tbsp red miso paste, or 1 tsp soy sauce
   or Marmite
400ml (14fl oz) vegetable stock
splash of Worcestershire sauce (optional)
approx. 250g (9oz) drained cooked or canned
   dark green or speckled lentils
2 tsp Dijon or wholegrain mustard
100ml (3½fl oz) double (heavy) cream
½ small bunch of tarragon, finely chopped
salt and freshly ground black pepper

This recipe is nutritionally supercharged, so much so I've also made the pastry a wholemeal one, but you can buy some good-quality ready-made pastry if you prefer. Within the remit of One Pan, cook the filling, then use the same pan to top with the pastry to bake, and it goes without saying, use a pan that is ovenproof. Once the filling is cooked, it is a good idea to let the pan cool a little before putting the pastry on top. Serve this pie with some good mustard, Dijon would be ideal. Use lentils that will hold their shape and not disintegrate too much. And use any mushrooms you like, from everyday field to more fancy varieties.

1. To make the pastry, tip the flours and a pinch of salt into a bowl, add the butter and rub it into the flour with your fingers until you have a breadcrumb texture. Alternatively, use a food processor to pulse. Add 3–4 tablespoons of ice-cold water and use a knife to stir until it starts to clump, then quickly bring together into a disc with your hands. Wrap and chill in the fridge for at least 25 minutes while you cook the filling.

2. In a shallow casserole or ovenproof frying pan over a moderate heat, cook the onion, leek, celery and carrot in the olive oil for 10 minutes until very soft. Stir in the garlic and thyme and cook for 1 minute until aromatic. Add the mushrooms and cook for 7–8 minutes until all the liquid has been released and then cooked away. Add the flour, tomato purée and miso and cook for 2 minutes, then stir in the stock and keep stirring until it comes to the boil to prevent any lumps. Reduce the heat and simmer for 5 minutes.

3. Remove from the heat and stir in the Worcestershire sauce (if using), the lentils, mustard, cream and tarragon, then season to taste with a little salt if needed (it should be quite well seasoned from the stock and miso) and a generous amount of pepper. Put to one side to cool a little.

4. Preheat the oven to 200°C/180°C fan/400°F/Gas 6.

5. Roll out the pastry to about 3mm (⅛in) thick and the same diameter as the pan (use the lid as a guide if it has one). Put the pastry lid on top of the lentil mixture in the pan and pierce the middle with a hole. Crimp the edges with a finger or fork to seal and brush with the beaten egg. Bake for 40 minutes until golden brown. Rest for 5 minutes before serving.

Pork Belly with Butter Beans and Sage

**Serves 4
(with leftovers
for cold cuts)**

1.5kg (3lb 5oz) pork belly, skin scored in
  thin lines
6 garlic cloves, 4 thinly sliced, 2 crushed to
  a paste
1 large bunch of sage, leaves picked, and
  ½ chopped
2 tsp ground fennel seeds
2 onions, thinly sliced
2 carrots, thinly sliced
2 leeks, trimmed, washed and thinly sliced
3 ripe tomatoes, roughly chopped
2 tbsp extra virgin olive oil
100ml (3½fl oz) dry white wine
approx. 500g (1lb 2oz) drained cooked or
  canned butter (lima) beans
300ml (10½fl oz) chicken or veg stock or water
sea salt and freshly ground black pepper

Make this dish as an alternative to your usual Sunday lunch, especially as it's the butter beans that are the star of the show here and this is a cookbook dedicated to beans, after all. In this recipe I suggest using butter beans, with a large surface area and soft skins, as they work especially well absorbing flavours when they wallow and soak in the cooking juices. Marinate the pork belly for at least a couple of hours or more, though however long you've got will help to ramp up the flavour. If you want to extend this dish to feed more of a crowd, in a more casual setting, my suggestion is to buy a load of good crusty rolls and serve slices of the pork belly and a big spoonful of the beans stuffed in the rolls to eat.

1. Season the pork belly all over with salt, the crushed garlic, the chopped sage, ground fennel and ½ teaspoon of black pepper, rubbing it into the skin in between the slashes and over the flesh. Allow to marinate for at least 1 hour in the fridge. Remove from the fridge at least 30 minutes before cooking.

2. Preheat the oven to 200°C/180°C fan/400°F/Gas 6.

3. Mix together all the vegetables, sliced garlic, tomatoes, olive oil and wine and season with salt and pepper. Set to one side.

4. Roast the pork in a large, deep roasting tin or ovenproof dish for 30 minutes until the pork is lightly coloured and crackled. Take the pork out of the roasting tin and tip in the vegetable mixture. Place the pork belly back on top and cover tightly with foil. Turn the oven down to 160°C/140°C fan/325°F/Gas 3 and cook for 1½–2 hours until the pork is easily pierced with a sharp knife.

5. When the cooking time's up, remove the foil and skim the excess fat from the surface of the cooking juices (although a bit is good for a little extra flavour). Add the beans, remaining sage and stock, stir through, re-cover with the foil and return to the oven for about 10 minutes to heat through.

6. Remove from the oven and rest somewhere warm for about 20 minutes, checking the seasoning of the vegetables and beans.

7. Transfer the cooked pork to a board and cut into thin slices. Serve with the vegetables and beans.

Slow Roast Lamb with Flageolet Beans, Thyme and Garlic

**Serves 4
(with leftovers
for cold cuts)**

1 tbsp honey

4 big thyme or rosemary sprigs, leaves picked

1 tbsp Dijon mustard

8 garlic cloves, 4 roughly chopped, 2 thinly
    sliced, 2 finely chopped

finely grated zest and juice of ½ unwaxed
    lemon

1kg (2lb 4oz) lamb (½ shoulder or leg, or
    4 lamb shanks, if you prefer)

2 large leeks, trimmed, washed and
    thinly sliced

150ml (5fl oz) dry white wine

200ml (7fl oz) boiling water

3 bay leaves

1 small bunch of parsley

approx. 250g (9oz) drained cooked or
    canned flageolet or white beans

salt and freshly ground black pepper

A slow-cooked shoulder of lamb is a delicious way of delivering a sensational but simple meal. Time is your best friend for this sort of cooking, as to get the best results you will need to cook the lamb slowly and at a lower temperature than a quicker roast when the lamb is served pink. You should also factor in a good long rest for the lamb after it has been cooked, for the meat to relax and turn tender. The upshot is this also gives you time to finish off any other cooking tasks before serving. This dish has a lot of garlic: in the lamb marinade, in the beans and, finally, sprinkled all over the top in the persillade to serve. As always, and with time on your side, it is wise to let the lamb marinate before cooking for as long as possible, ideally overnight.

1. Using a blender, combine the honey, thyme, mustard, roughly chopped garlic, the lemon zest and juice, ½ teaspoon of salt and a generous grind of pepper until you have a spreadable paste. Make deep incisions into the surface of the lamb, season with salt and rub the paste onto the lamb, pushing the marinade right into the incisions. Allow to marinate for at least 1 hour or overnight in the fridge. Remove from the fridge at least 30 minutes before cooking.

2. Preheat the oven to 200°C/180°C fan/400°F/Gas 6.

3. Transfer the lamb to a large casserole or roasting tray and put in the hot oven, uncovered, for 20 minutes to colour.

4. Add the leeks, sliced garlic, white wine, boiling water, bay leaves and a generous pinch of salt to the casserole. Cover with the lid or foil, drop the oven temperature to 180°C/160°C fan/350°F/Gas 4 and cook for 2–2½ hours until the lamb is very tender and able to be pulled apart with a fork. Check the liquid from time to time and top up with a little more boiling water if it dries out.

5. Just before the lamb comes out of the oven, finely chop the parsley and mix with the finely chopped garlic for the persillade.

6. When the lamb is cooked, remove to rest for at least 15 minutes. Skim off any excess fat from the surface of the cooking juices. Add the beans and, over a gentle heat on the hob or continuing in the oven, warm the beans through and check the seasoning.

7. Pull the lamb into thick slices or chunks and serve on top of the beans with any extra pan juices, sprinkled with the persillade.

Pot-roast Chicken with Cinnamon, Cardamom and Chickpeas

Serves 4

1 medium whole chicken
3 tbsp olive oil
½ tsp baharat (optional)
2 onions, thinly sliced
600ml (20fl oz) hot chicken stock or
  boiling water
4 garlic cloves, thinly sliced
4 bay leaves
1 unwaxed lemon, ½ very thinly sliced
2 cinnamon sticks
8 whole allspice berries
6 green cardamom pods, lightly crushed
200g (7oz) canned or fresh chopped tomatoes
approx. 250g (9oz) drained cooked or canned
  chickpeas (garbanzos)
1 small bunch of soft herbs, such as parsley,
  dill, coriander (cilantro), oregano, marjoram,
  mint or chives, roughly chopped
salt and freshly ground black pepper

Cinnamon, allspice and cardamom, together with the lemon and bay, give a gorgeous aroma to this pot-roast chicken. I'm a fan of adding thin slices of lemon to so many of the different dishes that I cook, braised, roasted or raw – I enjoy the intense lemony taste and also the texture the lemon brings. In this recipe especially, the chickpeas benefit from warming through in the spiced chicken cooking juices. I've suggested soft herbs to garnish, so you could use any or all of the following: parsley, dill, coriander, oregano, marjoram, mint or chives, though no one's going to mind if you end up using basil either, it's a bit more of a stretch with the baharat spice blend, but more than fine.

1. Preheat the oven to 180°C/160°C fan/350°F/Gas 4.

2. Rub the chicken with 1 tablespoon of the olive oil, ½ teaspoon of salt, some pepper and the baharat (if using) and place in a casserole or ovenproof dish on top of the onions. Pour over the remaining olive oil and half the chicken stock. Bake for 20–30 minutes until beginning to colour.

3. Remove the chicken from the dish and set aside on a plate.

4. Stir in the sliced garlic, bay leaves, lemon slices and whole spices, then add the tomatoes, chickpeas and the remaining chicken stock. Season to taste with salt and pepper.

5. Make a well in the middle of the chickpea mixture and place the chicken in it. Cover with the lid or foil and return to the oven. Cook for 30–45 minutes until the chicken is cooked and the sauce is rich and thick.

6. Stir the juice of the remaining lemon half, half the herbs and salt and pepper to taste into the chickpea mixture. Allow to rest for 10 minutes. Carve or joint the chicken and serve on top of the chickpeas, topped with the remaining herbs.

White Bean and Anchovy Stuffed Peppers

Serves 2 or 4

4 red (bell) peppers, halved and deseeded

approx. 250g (9oz) drained cooked or canned white beans

4 tbsp olive oil, plus more to serve

2 large garlic cloves, very thinly sliced

8 pitted kalamata olives, halved

1 small bunch of oregano, marjoram or basil, leaves picked

8 canned/jarred anchovies in oil, drained and halved

16 cherry tomatoes, halved

pinch of chilli flakes, plus more to serve

salt

I love anchovies, they are simply one of my very favourite ingredients. Add white beans and other fans of the anchovy, olive oil, red peppers, tomatoes and olives, and you're in for a real treat. The anchovies melt, buried in the beans, to give a deeply tasty, can't-quite-put-your-finger-on-it salty deliciousness, a perfect match for the creamy beans. This is a great starter, or alternatively, serve with good bread and a rocket salad for a light lunch or dinner. To up the ante, you could serve these bean-stuffed peppers on some bruschetta – good bread lightly toasted, then rubbed with raw garlic and drizzled with some extra virgin olive oil.

1. Preheat the oven to 180°C/160°C fan/350°F/Gas 4.

2. Line a roasting tray with baking paper and place the peppers, cut side-up, in the tray. Season inside each with salt, then divide the beans evenly between each pepper and drizzle the olive oil evenly among each half.

3. Evenly push the garlic, olives, half the herbs and the anchovies into the beans and top with the cherry tomato halves and chilli flakes.

4. Drizzle generously with more olive oil and roast for 30–35 minutes until the peppers have wilted and are cooked through.

5. Allow to cool until just warm or at room temperature and serve topped with the remaining herbs and a few more chilli flakes.

Harissa Roasted Cauliflower and Chickpea Traybake

Serves 4

150g (5½oz) plain yogurt (not Greek)

3 tbsp harissa paste

1 garlic clove, crushed

3 tbsp olive oil

1 whole cauliflower, leaves removed and stem trimmed

approx. 500g (1lb 2oz) drained cooked or canned chickpeas (garbanzos)

1 tsp coriander seeds

juice of 1 lemon

8 medjool dates, pitted and sliced

1 small bunch of parsley or mint, finely chopped

50g (1¾oz) walnuts, lightly toasted is ideal, finely chopped

30g (1oz) crispy fried onions

salt and freshly ground black pepper

Cauliflower feels like a much-revived ingredient and I think it's in no small part to the varied cooking methods that we now use, especially roasting and roasting whole. The caramelization that occurs when roasting cauliflower brings out the natural sugars and makes for more complex flavours, plus it's an easier way to introduce marinades and spices like in this recipe. The harissa-spiked yogurt creates a lovely crust over the cauliflower, and that is part of the basis for all the amazing textures and vibrant colours of this dish, with sticky chewy dates, crunchy walnuts, soft chickpeas, creamy yogurt, crispy fried onions and the bursts of flavour from the coriander seeds.

1. Preheat the oven to 200°C/180°C fan/400°F/Gas 6.

2. In a small bowl, mix 75g (2½oz) of the yogurt with half the harissa, the garlic, 1 tablespoon of the olive oil and ½ teaspoon of salt until well combined.

3. Place the whole cauliflower in a deep-lidded ovenproof pan about 25cm (10in) across. Season the cauliflower with pepper and brush the yogurt mixture all over the cauliflower, ensuring it's evenly coated.

4. Cover with a lid and roast the cauliflower for 25 minutes, then remove the lid and stir in the remaining harissa and olive oil, the chickpeas and coriander seeds and cook for another 15 minutes, or until the cauliflower is tender and golden brown.

5. While it's roasting, mix together the remaining yogurt and the lemon juice, and salt and pepper to taste.

6. Remove the caulifilower from the oven and let it cool slightly.

7. Sprinkle the parsley, walnuts, crispy onions and dates over the cauliflower and serve with the yogurt dressing.

Lentil, Pepper and Feta Cinnamon Filo Parcels

Makes 10

approx. 250g (9oz) drained cooked or canned
  dark green or speckled lentils
150g (5½oz) drained jarred roasted (bell)
  peppers, finely chopped
½ bunch of spring onions (scallions),
  finely chopped
1 small bunch of coriander (cilantro),
  finely chopped
150g (5½oz) feta, crumbled
100g (3½oz) walnuts or almonds, toasted
  and finely chopped
75g (2½oz) raisins
½ tsp ground cinnamon
¼ tsp ground ginger
pinch of ground nutmeg
pinch of ground cloves
finely grated zest of 1 unwaxed orange
10 sheets of filo pastry
75g (2½oz) butter, melted
salt and freshly ground black pepper

To serve
2 tbsp icing (confectioners') sugar
1 tsp ground cinnamon

Lentils make for a super and inexpensive filling for so many different pies and pastries. The texture and nutty, earthy flavour of the cooked lentils works well in this pastry. Here I am riffing on North African-style pastries called pastillas, a savoury pastry with a thin dusting of icing sugar, along with some ground cinnamon to serve. Savoury and sweet, it's a winning and brilliantly tasty combination. Singular pastries make for great packed lunch or picnic food, alternatively, make one single large pie by lining a baking dish with one-third of the filo, then fill with the lentil mixture before topping with the remaining filo, and bake until golden brown on top.

1. Preheat the oven to 180°C/160°C fan/350°F/Gas 4.

2. In a large bowl, combine the lentils with the peppers, spring onions, coriander, feta, walnuts and raisins. Add the ground spices and orange zest to the mixture. Mix well until all the ingredients are evenly combined and season to taste with salt and pepper.

3. Fold each filo sheet in three down their length, brushing with butter in between each layer. Place a spoonful of the filling towards the end of the pastry strip nearest you, slightly on the left of the strip and just up from the bottom.

4. Now fold the bottom right hand corner of the pastry strip up to cover the filling, then fold over the wrapped filling to give a triangular-shaped parcel.

5. Continue folding up the pastry strip, ensuring points are tucked in to prevent filling seepage. Brush the completed parcel with melted butter and place on a baking tray. Continue with the remaining filling and pastry strips.

6. Bake for 12–15 minutes, or until all the pastry strips are golden brown and crispy.

7. Once the pastries are baked, remove from the oven and let them cool for 15 minutes.

8. Dust with the icing sugar and cinnamon before serving just warm or at room temperature.

Baked Cod and Butter Beans with Aioli

Serves 4

1 fennel bulb, trimmed and thinly sliced

1 leek, trimmed, washed and thinly sliced

4 tbsp olive oil

2 garlic cloves, finely chopped

200ml (7fl oz) dry white wine

1 tsp ground fennel seeds

pinch of chilli flakes or chilli powder

a big pinch of saffron (optional)

2 thyme sprigs, leaves picked

2 bay leaves

2 strips of unwaxed orange zest, pith removed

600g (1lb 5oz) cherry tomatoes, halved

approx. 500g (1lb 2oz) drained cooked or canned butter (lima) beans

60g (2¼oz) kalamata or black olives, roughly chopped

4 firm cod or other white fish fillets, about 150g (5½oz) each

¼ small bunch of parsley, finely chopped

salt and freshly ground black pepper

For the aioli

1 egg yolk

1 garlic clove, crushed

1 tsp white wine vinegar or lemon juice

125ml (4fl oz) olive oil

pinch of Turkish chilli flakes, to serve (optional)

This is an oven-baked fish stew of sorts, and it's the type of dish that I love to serve with aioli to bring some real garlicky punch. This recipe leans on the complex layering of Mediterranean flavours like orange, fennel seeds, garlic, bay leaf and saffron, on top of some chopped tomatoes, along with the leek, fennel and white wine – combined it is these deliciously simple ingredients that create the base of the stew in which to cook the beans and fish. You could use any firm white fish for this dish, or even swap the fish for your favourite shellfish such as prawns. Keep an eye on the fish, it will cook relatively quickly in the stew. If you don't have time to make the aioli, use the best store-bought mayonnaise and season with crushed garlic.

1. For the aioli, in a small blender or food processor, or alternatively with a whisk and a bowl, mix the egg yolk, garlic and a good pinch of salt with the vinegar for about 30 seconds until thoroughly combined. Next, add 1 tablespoon of the olive oil in a thin, steady stream, with the motor running or continually whisking. Then continue to add the remaining oil in a thin stream, continually mixing or whisking to form a thick mayonnaise. Season with salt and pepper to taste and put to one side in a small bowl.

2. Preheat the oven to 190°C/170°C fan/375°F/Gas 5.

3. Mix the fennel and leek with 3 tablespoons of the olive oil and the garlic and season well with salt and pepper. Place in a good-sized ovenproof dish, in an even layer, then roast for about 20 minutes until softened and the edges have some colour.

4. Add the wine and return to the oven for 5 minutes, then stir in the spices, herbs, orange zest and cherry tomatoes and cook for 15–20 minutes until the tomatoes have broken down. Stir in the beans and olives and season to taste with salt and pepper.

5. Rub the fish fillets with the remaining olive oil and season with salt and pepper. Place the fish on top of the bean mixture and return the dish to the oven to roast for 8–10 minutes until the fish is cooked through and has turned opaque.

6. Remove from the oven, scatter over the chopped parsley and serve with a big spoon of aioli per portion of fish and a sprinkling of Turkish chilli flakes, to serve.

Gochujang Baked Beans with Kimchi

Serves 4

1 onion, finely diced

1 carrot, finely diced

2 celery stalks, finely diced

1 small red (bell) pepper, deseeded and finely diced

3 tbsp olive oil

3 garlic cloves, finely chopped

½ tsp smoked paprika

2 tsp soy sauce

3 tbsp gochujang paste

1 tbsp tomato purée (paste)

1 tbsp red wine vinegar

1 tbsp maple syrup or date syrup

approx. 750g (1lb 10oz) drained cooked or canned black or red kidney beans

1 bunch of spring onions (scallions), thinly sliced

salt and freshy ground black pepper

200g (7oz) sliced kimchi, to serve

There are so many options for baked bean recipes, so for this cookbook I needed to include a recipe good enough to compete with the ubiquitous, unbelievably popular, canned version but also interesting enough to stop you in your tracks – a recipe you simply have to make. This is it. Gochujang is a Korean chilli paste that is packed with umami and sweetness alongside considerable heat from the dried chilli flakes called gochugaru. Topping these luscious, fiery beans with a tangle of cold, straight-from-the-fridge kimchi is a winning combination. You can, in the spirit of one pan, then wipe out the pan, fry four eggs and serve them atop the beans for a breakfast, brunch, lunch or dinner fit for almost everyone and anyone.

1. Preheat the oven to 180°C/160°C fan/350°F/Gas 4.

2. In a casserole over a moderate heat, cook the onion, carrot, celery and red pepper in the olive oil for 10 minutes until soft.

3. Add the garlic and paprika and cook for 30 seconds, then stir in the soy sauce, gochujang, tomato purée, vinegar and syrup.

4. Stir in the beans and enough boiling water to create a thick sauce to loosely coat the beans. Bring to a simmer. Cover and place in the oven for 30 minutes. Stir in the spring onions and add salt and pepper to taste.

5. Serve topped with the kimchi.

SALADS

Niçoise Salad with Haricot Beans

Serves 4

4 eggs

300g (10½oz) green or runner beans, trimmed and cut into 4cm (1½in) lengths

approx. 750g (1lb 10oz) drained cooked or canned white beans, or haricot (navy) or flageolet beans

approx. 200g (7oz) canned tuna, drained weight (and do use the oil if it's extra virgin olive oil)

1 red onion, very thinly sliced

600g (1lb 5oz) ripe tomatoes, peeled and deseeded and roughly diced if large, or cherry tomatoes

1 cucumber, peeled, deseeded and roughly diced

1 green or red (bell) pepper, deseeded and roughly diced

120g (4¼oz) pitted kalamata olives, roughly chopped or halved

1 tbsp capers

1 big bunch of fresh oregano, leaves picked and larger leaves torn

For the dressing

1 garlic clove, crushed

6 canned/jarred anchovies, finely chopped (optional, but pretty key for me)

4 tbsp extra virgin olive oil

1½ tbsp red wine vinegar

salt and freshly ground black pepper

One of my favourite combinations: soft, pudgy white beans, anchovies and best-quality canned tuna, with some inky black olives, juicy ripe tomatoes, briny capers and more. Transportive is the dish that takes you someplace else other than your kitchen, plonking you by the seaside, somewhere warm and sunny. This recipe is just that. Peeling and deseeding the tomatoes is a happy task for me, and pleasing is the tomato skin as it peels back to show the tender pale flesh of the tomato, but, as with so much cooking, if you cannot be bothered to peel your tomatoes, don't worry about it, the world will still turn and your niçoise salad will still stop people in their tracks. This is the truth.

1. Put the eggs in a pan of cold water and bring slowly to the boil. Simmer for 8 minutes, adding the green beans after 3 minutes, then drain and put the eggs into cold water and the green beans to one side. Once cool enough to handle, peel the eggs, then halve and put to one side.

2. In a large bowl, mix all of the dressing ingredients together.

3. Toss the white beans, tuna, cooked green beans, onion, capers, oregano, black olives, tomatoes, cucumber and pepper together into the dressing and season to taste with salt and pepper. Allow the flavours to come together for 10 minutes, then give it all a gentle mix.

4. Serve topped with the hard boiled eggs, cut in half and seasoned well with freshly ground black pepper.

Lentil, Goat's Cheese and Mint Salad with Dates

Serves 4

2 onions, very finely diced
75ml (2½fl oz) olive oil
3 garlic cloves, very finely chopped
1½ tbsp red wine, white wine or cider vinegar
8 medjool dates, pitted and finely chopped
approx. 750g (1lb 10oz) drained cooked or
   canned green or speckled lentils
salt and freshly ground black pepper

To serve
150g (5½oz) soft goat's cheese, finely chopped
   or crumbled
1 small bunch of mint, leaves picked and
   roughly chopped

This lentil salad has appeared in a previous cookery book of mine, *Home Cookery Year*, but it's such a great combination that I am including it once more in this book – it really is that good and more people should make it. Perhaps what is most remarkable about the recipe is the unexpected combination of goat's cheese, good olive oil, chopped dates and fresh mint when served with the tender cooked earthy, nutty green lentils. Serve as an elegant salad as part of a wider sharing meal, or simply as a decadent light, but very beautiful lunch.

1. In a large frying pan over a medium heat, cook the onion in the olive oil for 10–15 minutes until very soft and beginning to turn golden brown.

2. Add the garlic and cook for 2–3 minutes until fragrant and golden, then remove from the heat and add the vinegar and dates.

3. Stir in the lentils, adding salt and pepper to taste, then serve topped with the goat's cheese and mint.

Borlotti Beans with Fennel, Orange and Kalamata Olives

Serves 4

1 small red onion, thinly sliced
2 tbsp red wine vinegar
approx. 500g (1lb 2oz) drained cooked or
   canned borlotti (cranberry) beans
4 medium oranges, peeled, plus
   1 extra orange for juice and zest
2 fennel bulbs, trimmed
80g (2¾oz) pitted kalamata olives, sliced
1 small bunch of flat-leaf parsley, roughly
   chopped
60ml (2fl oz) extra virgin olive oil
40g (1½oz) toasted walnuts, roughly chopped
salt and freshly ground black pepper

Fennel and orange salads bring a welcome dose of crisp winter sunshine to brighten cooler climate cookery. Red onion and walnuts work well with these two ingredients, all juicy, bitter and bright with aniseed flavours, and this cookery book being as it is a celebration of beans and pulses, I'm here to tell you white beans, in all their fulsome, creamy goodness are the best match for this seasonal salad. Seasoned assertively with good red wine vinegar and olive oil, this salad will eat better if left to wallow in the dressing for about 10 minutes, for the flavours to meld and really sing.

1. In a medium bowl, mix the red onion with the vinegar and leave to macerate for 5 minutes, then stir in the beans and the zest and juice of half an orange.

2. Remove the core from the fennel and cut into very thin wedges, reserving any fennel fronds to serve roughly chopped. Gently mix into the beans with the olives, parsley and olive oil and season to taste with salt and pepper.

3. Cut the peeled oranges into thin slices and arrange on a serving platter.

4. Spoon the bean mixture over the orange slices and sprinkle with the walnuts and any reserved fennel fronds.

Butter Beans with Endive, Celery and Smoked Mackerel

Serves 4

150g (5½oz) crème fraîche or plain yogurt
2 tsp Dijon mustard
finely grated zest and juice of 1 unwaxed lemon
4 tbsp olive oil
1 bunch of spring onions (scallions), thinly sliced
1 celery heart (pale inner trunk of celery, about 5 stalks), thinly sliced, leaves reserved
1 endive or Little Gem, leaves separated and roughly torn
approx. 750g (1lb 10oz) drained cooked or canned butter (lima) beans
3 smoked mackerel fillets, skin and bones removed and flesh roughly torn
40g (1½oz) toasted walnuts, roughly chopped
1 small bunch of herbs, ideally chervil, tarragon or chives, chopped
salt and freshly ground black pepper

Ah, a chopped salad of the finest sort, one that works brilliantly with that packet of smoked mackerel in the fridge and jar of butter (or any white) beans in the cupboard. I think endive gets overlooked here in the UK, stuck under a cloud of bitter and unpopular leaves – this needs to change. Endive is a terrific ingredient to have to hand for so many reasons – crisp, also crunchy, these pine-shaped, compact leaves are part of the chicory family. As salad leaves go, they are a robust salad with a relatively good shelf life. Here in this recipe, along with the butter beans, they make for a really memorable salad, perfectly dressed as they are with a spiky Dijon mustard and crème fraîche dressing.

1. In a serving bowl, mix the crème fraîche, mustard, lemon zest and juice and olive oil together with a little salt and pepper to taste.

2. Add the spring onions, celery (including the reserved leaves) and endive and mix well to coat with the dressing.

3. Top with the butter beans and mackerel, then scatter over the walnuts and herbs and serve immediately.

Whipped Butter Beans with Peppers, Smoked Almonds and Hot Honey

Serves 4
as a light lunch
or starter

150g (5½oz) jarred piquillo or roasted red (bell) peppers, drained and torn into pieces
2 tbsp olive oil
1 large rosemary sprig, leaves picked and finely chopped
approx. 750g (1lb 10oz) drained cooked or canned butter (lima) beans
1 garlic clove, finely chopped
30g (1oz) pumpkin seeds, toasted
50g (1¾oz) smoked almonds, roughly chopped
salt and freshly ground black pepper

For the hot honey
80g (2¾oz) honey
½–1 tsp chilli flakes
1 strip of unwaxed orange zest
½ cinnamon stick
juice of ½ orange

Right then, this is an eye-catching bean dish, so take your time to assemble this gorgeous collection of ingredients as beautifully as you can. Making your own hot honey is a cinch, and while you can flavour honey with all number of different ingredients, I'm suggesting orange zest, chilli flakes and cinnamon here as an especially flattering combination to work alongside the smoked almonds, roasted jarred peppers and, yes of course, the creamy blanket of ultra-smooth blitzed butter beans flavoured with garlic and olive oil.

1. In a small pan, heat the honey with the chilli flakes, orange zest and cinnamon stick until bubbling at the edges, then stir through the orange juice and put to one side.

2. Mix the red peppers with 1 tablespoon of the olive oil, half the rosemary and salt and pepper to taste. Put to one side.

3. In a blender, blend about 90 per cent of the beans (keeping the remainder whole to garnish), the garlic, the remaining olive oil, the remaining rosemary and salt and pepper to taste.

4. Spread the whipped beans on plates or a platter and top with the rosemary-scented peppers. Top with the pumpkin seeds, smoked almonds and remaining whole beans and drizzle over the hot honey.

Chickpeas with Green Olives, Preserved Lemon and Coriander

Serves 4

2 onions, thinly sliced

4 tbsp extra virgin olive oil

2 garlic cloves, thinly sliced

½ tsp ground turmeric

2 tsp harissa paste, plus more to serve

approx. 750g (1lb 10oz) drained cooked or canned chickpeas (garbanzos)

1 preserved lemon, pips removed, skin and flesh finely chopped

20 green olives, pitted and finely chopped

80g (2¾oz) baby spinach leaves

1 small bunch of coriander (cilantro), roughly chopped

juice of 1 lemon

salt and freshly ground black pepper

20g (¾oz) flaked almonds, to garnish

Hands down, preserved or salted lemons are one of my favourite storecupboard ingredients (along with many different beans and pulses, of course!). What preserved lemons bring to a dish is a turbo-charged lemony-ness that is unrivalled. Fresh lemon can also be used in conjunction with preserved lemon, the two lemon profiles only complementing each other even further. So here we have a bright, fresh, salty, lemony flavour, one of the best matches around for this salad of chubby chickpeas, green olives, spinach and coriander, pepped up with a big spoonful of fiery harissa.

1. In a large frying pan over a moderate heat, cook the onions in the olive oil for 10–15 minutes until very soft and beginning to colour.

2. Add the garlic, turmeric and harissa and cook for 1 minute until fragrant. Remove from the heat and stir in the chickpeas.

3. Mix the chickpea and cooked onion mixture with the remaining ingredients, adding salt and pepper to taste. Scatter over the almonds and coriander and blob over extra harissa. Serve at room temperature or cold.

Black Beans with Burnt Salsa and Tortilla Chips

Serves 4

3 medium tomatoes

2 garlic cloves, peeled

1 small red onion, quartered

2 limes, 1 cut into wedges

1–3 tsp chipotle chilli paste, to taste

1 small bunch of coriander (cilantro), leaves picked and finely chopped

approx. 750g (1lb 10oz) drained cooked or canned black beans

100g (3½oz) radishes, thinly sliced

2 avocados, peeled, stoned and diced

1 small bag of blue or yellow tortilla chips (approx. 75g/2½oz)

salt and freshly ground black pepper

To serve

150g (5½oz) feta, crumbled

1–2 fresh jalapeño chillies, thinly sliced, or hot sauce (optional)

big pinch chilli flakes or Tajin spice mix

Taking inspiration here from Mexican recipes for chilaquiles, a sometimes breakfast (though I'd eat it any time) dish of fried corn tortillas drenched and simmered in a salsa until softened just so and served with crumbled cheese, fresh chilli and chopped coriander. This version is very much one-pan so instead of frying tortillas I am using tortilla chips all tossed together with the burnt salsa. I'm also adding black beans to my salsa, because, well, you know… If you wanted to wipe out your pan and fry an egg to top your tortilla chips, then, yes, you absolutely could. One-pan beans, just add an egg!

1. Dry-fry or grill the tomatoes, garlic cloves and onion for 10 minutes until lightly charred all over. Leave to cool slightly, then peel and finely chop all together. Mix in the juice of 1 lime, the chipotle and half the coriander.

2. Stir through the beans, radishes and avocado and season to taste with salt and pepper.

3. Just before serving, stir through the tortilla chips and serve topped with the remaining coriander, the feta and fresh chillies (if using) and chilli flakes with the lime wedges on the side.

Black-eyed Bean Greek Salad

Serves 4

1 red onion, very thinly sliced

2 tbsp red wine vinegar

1 cucumber, peeled and cut into bite-sized cubes (deseeded if you like)

6 ripe tomatoes, diced

20 kalamata olives (pitted if you prefer)

1 small bunch of flat-leaf parsley, roughly chopped

approx. 500g (1lb 2oz) drained cooked or canned black-eyed beans (black-eyed peas)

4 tbsp olive oil

½ tsp dried oregano

200g (7oz) feta, in a single piece or diced

salt and freshly ground black pepper

A good Greek salad is absolutely one of my favourite and most simple dishes to make and also to eat. The caveat being, it needs to be a blazing hot and sunny day to eat your Greek salad, for this is the route to pure happiness. The tomatoes must be super ripe and juicy, accompanied by good feta cheese, kalamata olives and crunchy, glistening cucumber – and seasoning the mix properly is key. Black-eyed beans are opular in many different cuisines throughout the world, I enjoy their diminutive shape and the two-tone appearance – they are a terrific addition to this Greek Salad to say the least.

1. In a bowl, rub a big pinch of salt into the onion, then pour over the vinegar and put to one side.

2. In a large bowl, mix together the cucumber, tomatoes, olives, parsley and black-eyed beans, then mix in the onion mixture, half the olive oil and half the oregano. Season to taste with salt and pepper (remembering the feta will add salt).

3. Serve topped with the feta, sprinkled with the remaining oregano and drizzled with the remaining olive oil.

Roasted Vegetables with Borlotti Beans and Fennel Yogurt

Serves 4

1 red onion, chopped into 4cm (1½in) dice

1 large fennel bulb, trimmed and thinly sliced, any fronds reserved and finely chopped

1 large sweet potato, peeled and thinly sliced

2 large carrots, thinly sliced

2 raw beetroots (beets), peeled and thinly sliced

4 tbsp olive oil

1 small garlic clove

350g (12oz) plain yogurt

juice of ½ lemon

1 tsp fennel seeds, toasted and crushed

approx. 500g (1lb 2oz) drained cooked or canned borlotti (cranberry) beans

½ bunch of dill (or use more fennel fronds), finely chopped

30g (1oz) toasted pine nuts

salt and freshly ground black pepper

Roasted vegetables seems like a vague missive from me in the title for this recipe and, sure enough, I do give you a hit list of vegetables to roast, but do take this with a pinch of salt. Roast your favourite combination of veg, or whatever you have to hand. I am a big fan of clearing out the veg drawer in my fridge and roasting the lot with salt, spices and olive oil until soft and burnished, then all you have to do is add some flattering ingredients and plate the lot as attractively as you can to serve. This is where borlotti beans and this gem of a dressing come in handy; seasoning and thinning the yogurt with fennel seeds, crushed garlic and lemon juice really brings this medley of roasted veg to life, then just add the beans!

1. Preheat the oven to 190°C/170°C fan/375°F/Gas 5.

2. In a large bowl, toss the onion, fennel, sweet potato, carrots and beetroots with the olive oil and season with salt and pepper.

3. Transfer to 1–2 baking sheets in an even layer and roast the vegetables for 20 minutes until tender and golden.

4. While the veg is roasting, crush the garlic with salt and add to the yogurt with the lemon juice and crushed fennel seeds, along with any reserved fennel fronds, adding more salt and pepper to taste.

5. Stir the beans into the roasting vegetables and return to the oven to warm through for 3–4 minutes.

6. Spread the yogurt on plates or a platter and top with the vegetables, the dill (or more fennel fronds) and toasted pine nuts.

Salad of Lentils, Radicchio, Pickled Walnuts and Prunes

Serves 4

approx. 750g (1lb 10oz) drained cooked or
   canned green or speckled lentils
1 celery heart, stalks and leaves, thinly sliced
1 small head of radicchio, thinly sliced
3 spring onions (scallions), thinly sliced
1 small bunch of flat-leaf parsley,
   roughly chopped
80g (2¾oz) pickled walnuts, thinly sliced
80g (2¾oz) pitted prunes, chopped

For the dressing
4 tbsp extra virgin olive oil
2 tbsp balsamic vinegar
1 tsp Dijon mustard
salt and freshly ground black pepper

One for the winter months, when the veg stalls and markets (and supermarkets for that matter) all have a bright, beautiful array of radicchio on their counters. I have seen people buy armfuls of radicchio, and other Italian chicories, in lieu of roses come Valentine's Day, and what a bouquet they make! I certainly know which armful of pink I'd prefer to be handed. I love radicchio, I love everything about it, I love the tender, furled leaves, the savoury bitter quality that lends itself so perfectly to sweet, creamy, salty ingredients, and I love it most of all when matched with lentils, these tiny edible seeds from the legume plant nestling in the pink and ruffled leaves. In fact, buy radicchio and make this salad for someone you love.

1. In a large bowl, mix together the lentils, celery, radicchio, spring onions, parsley, pickled walnuts and prunes.

2. In a separate small bowl, whisk together the olive oil, balsamic vinegar and mustard and season with salt and pepper.

3. Mix the dressing into the salad and mix until well combined. Season to taste with salt and pepper. Allow the salad to sit for 5 minutes to let the flavours come together, then serve.

Roasted Cauliflower with Raisins, Almonds, White Beans and Chimichurri

Serves 4

1 medium cauliflower, core removed and trimmed and thinly sliced, the rest cut into florets
1 large red onion, thinly sliced into wedges
3 tbsp olive oil
½ tsp smoked paprika
1 tsp ground cumin
60g (2¼oz) raisins
approx. 500g (1lb 2oz) drained cooked or canned white beans
50g (1¾oz) flaked almonds
salt and freshly ground black pepper

For the chimichurri
1 small bunch of parsley
2 garlic cloves, finely chopped
50ml (1¾fl oz) olive oil
2 tbsp red wine vinegar
½–1 tsp chilli flakes
pinch of dried oregano

Chimichurri is an Argentinian green sauce made with fresh parsley, dried oregano, chilli flakes and red wine vinegar among other ingredients. It is one of the best green sauces going and, once you have a recipe for it, and know how quick and delicious it is to make, you'll be spooning chimichurri over everything, mark my words. In this warm jumble of a salad, for it is absolutely a salad, the chickpeas work beautifully with the plump raisins, almonds and spiced and roasted cauliflower and red onion wedges. Enjoy.

1. Preheat the oven to 200°C/180°C fan/400°F/Gas 6.

2. Toss the cauliflower and red onion with the olive oil, paprika, cumin and some salt and pepper. Spread them on a baking sheet and roast for 25–30 minutes, or until golden brown and tender.

3. While the cauliflower is cooking, in a small heatproof bowl, soak the raisins in enough boiling water to cover for 5 minutes.

4. For the chimicurri, blend, or finely chop by hand, the parsley and garlic, then blend (or stir) in the olive oil, red wine vinegar, chilli flakes, dried oregano and salt and pepper to give a smoothish sauce.

5. In a large bowl, combine the roasted cauliflower and red onion with the chickpeas, drained raisins and the almonds. Season to taste with salt and pepper.

6. Drizzle the chimichurri over the salad and scatter the almonds to serve.

Chana Chaat

approx. 750g (1lb 10oz) drained cooked or
    canned chickpeas (garbanzos)
1 cucumber, peeled, deseeded and finely
    chopped
1 red onion, very finely chopped
2 large ripe tomatoes, finely chopped
1 green chilli, finely chopped (optional)
2 tsp chaat masala
salt and freshly ground black pepper

For the tamarind dressing
4 tbsp tamarind paste
juice of ½ lemon
2 tsp sugar
½ tsp ground cumin

To serve
60g (2¼oz) plain yogurt (not Greek)
40g (1½oz) sev
1 small bunch of coriander (cilantro),
    roughly chopped

I often talk about building layers of flavours in my cooking, integrating different ingredients to combine into one particular dish. I can't think of a better example of this sophisticated cookery practice than here in this recipe for chana chaat. Legumes are the star of the show here, chickpeas in particular, but, really, they are nothing without their supporting cast of diced tomatoes, red onion, green chilli and cucumber. Another layer of complexity comes with the addition of chaat masala, which is central to a good chaat and can easily be purchased online and in Indian stores or bigger supermarkets with an international aisle. Sour and spicy, it's a winning spice blend to have to hand. Travelling through India, I was always so in awe of the many chaat vendors and just how different the variety of chaats on offer were up and down this vast and beautiful country. Serve as a side dish or on its own – crunchy and juicy, this is quite simply one of the best salads out there.

1. In a large bowl, mix together the chickpeas with the cucumber, onion, tomatoes, green chilli (if using) and chaat masala, then season to taste with salt and pepper. Put to one side for the flavours to come together for 10 minutes.

2. Whisk together the tamarind dressing ingredients, adding salt to taste.

3. Put the chickpea mixture on plates or a large platter and top with the yogurt, tamarind dressing and sev, then sprinkle over the chopped coriander.

SNACKS & DIPS

Roasted Garlic Hummus

Serves 4

1 whole garlic bulb
1 tbsp sesame seeds
40ml (1½fl oz) olive oil
big pinch of ground turmeric
approx. 250g (9oz) drained cooked or canned
  chickpeas (garbanzos)
100g (3½oz) light tahini paste
juice of ½ lemon
1 tsp Urfa chilli flakes, or use your favourite
  chilli flakes
salt
1 tbsp za'atar, to serve
breadsticks, flatbreads or crackers, to serve

Slow roasting garlic tempers its powerful character to an extent that means you can use it in relatively large quantities in recipes, which is what we all want, right? The softened flesh can then be squeezed out and you'll find it has become deeply savoury, as well as wonderfully sweet. Whizzed up in this hummus recipe the roasted garlic lends a silky soft texture, boosting flavour. It's best to try and find large and tender chickpeas for this, not only for their creamier consistency, but also, the larger the chickpea, the fewer skins you'll have to remove and I recommend you do remove the skins in this recipe for a super smooth hummus*. Sesame seeds bring crunch and an attractive speckle when serving this hummus. As for the za'atar – a fabulous spice blend combining sumac, cumin, salt, sesame and oregano, sometimes thyme – it's a wonderful condiment to use liberally and often on dips, roasted vegetables and flatbreads.

* To be honest removing the skins is optional if you don't have the patience, but it will make the finished hummus smoother and silkier.

1. Preheat the oven to 180°C/160°C fan/350°F/Gas 4.

2. Wrap the garlic bulb in foil in a small ovenproof dish and roast for 20–25 minutes until soft and sweet. Squeeze the roasted flesh out of the papery skins and put in a food processor.

3. Place the sesame seeds in the same ovenproof dish and toast in the oven for 2–4 minutes until golden brown. Stir in the olive oil and turmeric and put to one side.

4. Tip three-quarters of the chickpeas onto a clean tea towel and gently roll to remove as many of the skins as you have the patience for, discarding the skins.

5. Put the skinned chickpeas in a food processor, along with the tahini, lemon juice, a big pinch of salt and the roasted garlic flesh. Process until the chickpeas are a rough purée, then, with the motor still running, add enough cold water, bit by bit, to give you the consistency of whipped double cream.

6. To serve, spread the hummus on a plate and drizzle over the sesame and olive oil, covering the surface of the hummus, then sprinkle over the remaining chickpeas, chilli flakes and za'atar.

Whipped White Beans with Rosemary and Crudités

Serves 4

50ml (1¾fl oz) extra virgin olive oil
2 garlic cloves, thinly sliced
pinch of chilli flakes, plus more to serve
2 rosemary sprigs, leaves picked and finely
  chopped, plus a few extra small sprigs
  to serve
approx. 250g (9oz) drained cooked or canned
  cannellini beans
finely grated zest and juice of ½ unwaxed
  lemon
salt and freshly ground black pepper
crackers and breadsticks, to serve

For the crudités

1 fennel bulb, trimmed and cut into
  thin wedges
6 small carrots, cut in half lengthways
1 celery heart, pale stalks with leaves,
  separated
1 endive, leaves separated
lettuce leaves
radishes, cut in half lengthways

Cannellini beans have a thin skin and creamy flesh that is ideal for blending into a whipped, light and creamy dip, perfect here with raw vegetable crudités to swoosh through then chomp on. Thinner skinned beans also means no need for peeling as in the hummus recipe on page 140. Cannellini beans love good-quality extra virgin olive oil. In this recipe, the olive oil is gently infused with garlic, chilli and rosemary, all giving a gentle but persuasive lift to the flavours of the blended beans. I suggest raw vegetable crudités here to serve; equally so, on toasted bread all rubbed with raw garlic and more olive oil is equally delicious. Moving beyond the realm of a one-pan cookbook, this cannellini bean dip is a fabulous accompaniment to grilled or roasted lamb or chicken as well as fish, such as barbecued trout or scallops, and of course, all roasted, grilled or barbecued vegetable-centric dishes.

1. In a small pan over a low heat, gently heat the olive oil with the garlic, chilli flakes and half the rosemary until it just begins to bubble. Remove from the heat and put to one side to infuse.

2. Place the beans and the remaining rosemary in a food processor or blender with the lemon zest and juice and blend to a smooth purée. Season to taste with salt and pepper.

3. Transfer the bean mixture to a small bowl. Strain in the rosemary and garlic oil, mix well and top with more chilli flakes and a few sprigs of rosemary. Serve with the crudités and crackers alongside.

Roasted Peanut Butter, Maple Syrup and Chipotle Chickpeas

Serves 4

approx. 500g (1lb 2oz) drained cooked or canned chickpeas (garbanzos)
1 tbsp runny smooth peanut butter
1 tsp maple syrup or honey
2 tsp soy sauce
1 tsp cider or white wine vinegar
1 tbsp chipotle chilli paste
pinch of salt
2 tbsp olive oil

Roasting chickpeas until crispy makes them incredibly moreish, and they are a great snack to munch on in front of a film – superior even to popcorn? I've given these chickpeas a drain and a quick pat dry, then drenched the lot in a mix of peanut butter, maple syrup, soy sauce and vinegar with a generous measure of chipotle chilli paste for added pep. As combinations go, this is a winning one. As with other recipes, I recommend you source the large, soft chickpeas to roast; try to avoid the smaller, harder varieties that you sometimes come across with more budget brands, as when roasted it is these chickpeas that turn a little hard and bullet-like when in contact with the dry heat of the oven – better to use these smaller sort in any wet and soupy preparations.

1. Preheat the oven to 210°C/190°C fan/410°F/Gas 6½. Line an oven tray (big enough to take the chickpeas in a single layer) with baking paper. Alternatively, you can use an air fryer for this recipe as chickpeas air-fry especially well – air-fry in short bursts on a high heat (follow the instructions on your air fryer).

2. Pat the chickpeas dry on a clean tea towel and then mix the chickpeas in a bowl with all the remaining ingredients.

3. Place in the lined oven tray, spreading out the chickpeas in a single layer. Roast until golden brown and crisp, about 20–25 minutes (depending on size), shaking the tray a few times through the cooking so the chickpeas coat in the spices and roast evenly in the tray.

4. Check the seasoning and serve immediately or at room temperature, although they will lose a bit of crispness as they cool. I like them both ways!

Edamame Guacamole

Serves 4

350g (12oz) frozen edamame beans, shelled and defrosted

3–5 tbsp olive oil, or ideally use avocado or macadamia nut oil

juice of 1 big lime

½ small red onion, very finely diced

1 tomato, peeled, cored and very finely diced

1 fresh jalapeño, finely chopped (optional)

1 small bunch of coriander (cilantro), leaves picked and finely chopped

salt and freshly ground black pepper

corn/tortilla chips, to serve

I buy the odd avocado as my kids all like eating guacamole. The veg shops close to my home all topple with avocados in various states of usability – some rock hard, some perfectly ripe, and some frankly rotten. It's a bit of a lottery, and supermarket avocados seem to suffer the same fate. I wanted to include a recipe in this, the bean snacking chapter, for a guacamole (of sorts) which uses beans to ape avocados in a guacamole. Step forward edamame, all green, soft and creamy, a great match for avocado. Edamame are young soybeans harvested before they ripen or harden, they are soft and blend rather well. You can buy them frozen in pods, simply defrost and then briefly blanch or steam to then drench in soy sauce. Sucking beans from pods will always be a favourite beany snack for me and my kids, but should you also have a household of guacamole fans, then make this – buy a bag of podded edamame beans and away you go. The spiky, fresh and fiery salsa on top of the edamame guacamole really makes this dish sing. Serve with corn/tortilla chips to shovel; alternatively, serve as a condiment to tacos or on toast.

1. Cook the edamame beans in boling water or according to the packet instructions, then drain and place in cold water to refresh until cool.

2. Blend three-quarters of the edamame beans with the oil and half the lime juice and season to taste with salt and pepper. Put to one side.

3. Mix the remaining edamame with the red onion, tomato, jalapeño (if using) and coriander, then stir through the remaining lime juice and season to taste with salt and pepper.

4. Serve the guacamole topped with the tomato salsa and with corn/tortilla chips on the side.

Puy Lentil and Olive Tapenade

Serves 4

80g (2¾oz) pitted kalamata olives

1 garlic clove, thinly sliced

2 canned/jarred anchovies in oil, drained and finely chopped (optional)

1 thyme sprig, leaves picked

1 tbsp capers

approx. 100g (3½oz) drained cooked or canned Puy or dark green or speckled lentils

75ml (2½fl oz) olive oil

1 tsp finely grated unwaxed orange or lemon zest

squeeze of orange or lemon juice, to taste

salt and freshly ground black pepper

Tapenade is a terrific condiment to have on hand, instantly lending a burst of briny, inky olive flavour to so many different dishes. For this recipe, I'm adding some small Puy, dark green or speckled lentils to the usual assembly of tapenade ingredients. I find the earthy, nutty flavours of dark lentils work really well in a tapenade, don't blitz them, just mix them through at the end, as they give a gorgeous loose texture to the finished tapenade. Have this smothered thickly on a slice of toast for a speedy, fulfilling snack, or, taking you beyond the remit of one pan, use the tapenade as a condiment to roast lamb, chicken or grilled oily fish, or with grilled and roasted vegetables, or spooned onto pizza, or slather in sandwiches as the ultimate flavour boost.

1. Put the olives, garlic, anchovies (if using), half the thyme and capers in a food processor and pulse until you have a coarse paste, or finely chop them all on a board. Stir in the lentils.

2. Place in a bowl and mix in the olive oil, remaining thyme and orange/lemon zest, adding salt, the orange/lemon juice and some pepper to taste.

Lentil, Yogurt and Courgette Dip with Walnuts

Serves 4

2 firm medium courgettes (zucchini), coarsely grated – if larger, remove the seedy middle
4 tbsp olive oil
1 garlic clove, crushed
3 spring onions (scallions), finely chopped
finely grated zest and juice of ½ unwaxed lemon
250g (9oz) Greek yogurt
approx. 200g (7oz) drained cooked or canned Puy or dark green or speckled lentils
50g (1¾oz) walnuts, roughly crushed
1 small bunch of dill, roughly chopped
chilli flakes – dark ones like Urfa are nice (optional)
salt and freshly ground black pepper
flatbreads, to serve

This mezze-style dip is a gorgeous one. The silky-soft grated and cooked courgettes mixed through with the Greek yogurt and lentils is such a great combination. Just add walnuts, one of my favourite of all nuts, chopped and scattered over to serve. Do try and source some Turkish chilli flakes for this recipe, I'm a fan of dark, fruity chilli flakes such as Urfa flakes for something like this, hotter even still would be Aleppo flakes. Most supermarkets seem to stock both these days, if not, head to a Mediterranean or Middle Eastern store and ask there. Drizzle over with good extra virgin olive oil and serve with warm flatbreads to scoop.

1. In a large bowl, mix the courgettes with a big pinch of salt and leave for 5 minutes, then use your hands to squeeze out any excess water.

2. In a large frying pan over a moderate heat, fry the courgettes in 2 tablespoons of the olive oil for 5 minutes or so until the courgettes have softened, then stir in the garlic and spring onions and cook for 1 minute until fragrant. Remove from the heat and spread on a plate to cool.

3. When the courgettes are cool, put them in a mixing bowl and stir in the lemon zest and juice, yogurt and lentils and season to taste with salt and pepper.

4. Serve spread out on a plate, topped with the walnuts, dill, the remaining olive oil and the chilli flakes (if using), with flatbreads to accompany.

Pickled Snacking Beans

Serves 4

approx. 500g (1lb 2oz) drained cooked or canned butter (lima) beans

For the pickle
110ml (3¾fl oz) water
110ml (3¾fl oz) white wine vinegar
20g (¾oz) caster sugar
1 garlic clove, sliced
2 bay leaves
1 thyme sprig
½ tsp salt
1 small red onion, thinly sliced
1 tsp coriander seeds
1 tsp black peppercorns
1 tsp nigella seeds
1 dried red chilli, sliced
2 strips of unwaxed lemon zest

These are lovely, and just the thing to put out on a plate, perhaps with some toothpicks as antipasti, to serve with drinks before a meal. The pickle solution has a fair bit going on, but nothing hard to track down – what all these ingredients bring is a wonderful aromatic, sharp, sweet flavour for the beans to pickle in. Much like lupin beans scooped from large tubs onto little serving plates as a snack to a cold beer in so many Mediterranean countries, these pickled beans are a great way to sharpen your appetite and get you in the mood for the meal ahead. Try to source the best quality beans for this, ideally butter beans or other white beans. Stored in the fridge, the beans will last for up to a week.

1. Add all of the pickle ingredients to a pan and bring to the boil, then remove from the heat and allow to infuse and cool.

2. Put the beans in a large sterilized jar.

3. Pour the spiced vinegar and all the flavourings over the beans in the jar and seal. Give the jar a gentle shake to ensure the beans are fully surrounded by the pickle.

4. Keep in the fridge and pickle overnight, allowing the pickled beans to come to room temperature before serving. They keep in the fridge for up to a week.

Lentil, Seed and Pepper Crackers

Makes 18–26 crackers

150g (5½oz) drained cooked or canned dark
 green or speckled lentils
100g (3½oz) wholemeal (wholewheat) flour, plus
 more to roll (or use a 50/50 blend of plain
 (all-purpose) and wholemeal flour)
50g (1¾oz) butter, softened
¼ tsp freshly cracked black pepper
2 tsp caraway seeds
flaky sea salt

The cooked and blitzed lentils in these crackers give a wonderful nutty flavour to the cracker dough. By all means play around with the combination of seeds used – it's worth noting though, that if you use bigger seeds, it's best to give them a coarse crush before adding them to the cracker dough, too big and the dough will tear when you come to roll it. I've used caraway seeds in the crackers, but whole cumin or cracked coriander seeds would also work. Serve these crackers with some of the soup or dip recipes given in the book; they are also great with a slice of cheese and spoonful of chutney or mustard. Alternatively, just eat them as they are. Stored in an airtight tin, the crackers will keep for up to a week.

1. Preheat the oven to 180°C/160°C fan/350°F/Gas 4 and line a baking sheet with baking paper.

2. In a food processor, blend the lentils to a smooth paste.

3. Mix the lentil paste with the flour, butter, pepper and half the caraway seeds. If required, add a couple of tablespoons of water to bring the dough together, then roll into a ball of dough.

4. Place the dough on a lightly floured surface and roll it out to 2–3mm (¹⁄₁₆–⅛in) thick. Sprinkle with the remaining caraway seeds and some flaky salt and press into the dough.

5. Use a knife or pizza wheel to cut the dough into desired shapes.

6. Place the cut crackers on the prepared baking sheet, leaving a bit of space between each one, and bake for 12–15 minutes, or until the edges are golden brown and they are cooked through and dry.

7. Allow the crackers to cool on the baking sheet for a few minutes before transferring them to a wire rack to cool completely. Store in an airtight container.

Lentil Empanadas

Makes 8

330g (11½oz) plain (all-purpose) flour
½ tsp baking powder
100g (3½oz) cold butter, diced
120g (4¼oz) drained cooked or canned green
  or brown lentils
2 tbsp olive oil
60g (2¼oz) good-quality red pesto
80g (2¾oz) soft goat's cheese or ricotta,
  crumbled
60g (2¼oz) pitted black or green olives, finely
  chopped (kalamata are good)
½ small bunch of parsley, leaves picked and
  finely chopped
½ bunch of spring onions (scallions), very
  finely chopped
salt
oil, for frying
hot sauce, to serve (optional)

Make these empanadas as a snack or lunch to pack and eat on the go. Fillings for empanadas are numerous; for a really good empanada, you're after a few different textures and bursts of flavours in the filling, ensuring each bite is a tantalizing one. Lentils work beautifully here, but you could just as well switch them out for some black beans or black-eyed beans, for example. I would recommend, and I often do, a bit of hot sauce dashed over the top to serve. You can bake them at 180°C/160°C fan/350°F/Gas 4 for 35–40 minutes until golden brown instead of frying, but honestly, it's the fried, flaky exterior that makes these empanadas especially unbeatable.

1. Mix the flour, baking powder and ½ teaspoon of salt and the baking powder in a food processor or bowl.

2. Add the pieces of butter and pulse until mixed or, if using a bowl, rub in with your fingertips until the mixture resembles breadcrumbs.

3. Add 200ml (7fl oz) of water and mix to a soft dough, then knead until smooth, adding a bit more flour if it is too sticky. Cover in a bowl and allow to rest for at least 30 minutes.

4. Meanwhile, in a bowl, gently mash half the lentils with the olive oil and red pesto to a very coarse purée, then stir through the remaining lentils, the cheese, olives, parsley and spring onions.

5. Roll out the dough to about 3mm (⅛in) thick and cut out 8 discs, each about 16cm (6¼in) in diameter (re-rolling any trimmings, if needed). Spoon some cheese filling onto the centre of each disc.

6. Fold the discs in half and seal the edges, pressing gently with your fingertips, then using a fork to press down and seal. Chill the empanadas in the fridge for at least 30 minutes.

7. Heat about 3cm (1¼in) of oil in a deep, wide frying pan over a moderate heat, until an added piece of dough sizzles, then carefully fry the empanadas for about 1–2 minutes per side until they are golden on each side.

8. Drain on kitchen paper and serve straight away, with hot sauce (if using).

Index